NO TI
FOR TE

GH01033762

Recollections of a Cornish childhood

by

Des Philp

DYLLANSOW TRURAN

Published by Dyllansow Truran
Trewolsta
Trewirgie
Redruth
Kernow

ISBN 1 85022 098 0

Typeset by Kestrel Data, Exeter
Printed and bound in Great Britain by Short Run Press Ltd, Exeter

Contents

	Preface	vii
1	The very early years	1
2	A time for learning	9
3	Boy in the chair	13
4	Sunday School	16
5	The Painting	20
6	'O God take me home'	24
7	Mary Wall	27
8	Passing Thro'	31
9	Legend of Arnold	35
10	'I'll have my supper now'	48
11	Found drowned	52
12	Ad Astra	56
13	Late Lamented	59
14	Taxi!	62
15	Against all odds	66
16	Garden serenade	69
17	Regatta	78
18	Wreckers	89
19	The Seafarers	95
20	'Clouds and darkness are around him'	119
21	The 'Moloch'	127
22	One day at a time	131
23	Nothing Sacred	145
24	'Creatures litt'ler than thou'	150
25	The quiet man	155
26	A story to tell	159
27	'Coming Soon'	164
28	Salad Days	176
	Conclusion	201

The author. 1933

Acknowledgements

The Everyman Dictionary of Quotations & Proverbs
  (J. M. Dent & Sons).
Penguin Book of Hymns (Penguin).
Concise Oxford Dictionary of Quotations (O.U.P.).
Quotations from the 'Holy Bible', Auth. Version (C.U.P.)
Chorus: 'My Old Pal of Yesterday' (Peer Music).
Hayle & Phillack Homeland Handy guide, No. 24 (circa 1911).

For the loan of photographs, my thanks to: Keith Harris, Barrie Allen, Florence Thomas, Lillian Penberthy, Cyril Stevens, Roselene Davey, Christina Thomas, George Williams, Russell Williams, Cynthia Smith, Lily Hosken, May Perry. The photograph of T. J. Porter, was taken from his booklet 'Holidays in Cornwall' (circa 1920) Pub. T. J. Porter.

I am also indebted to: Ralph Pearce (St Just), Andrew Nicholls, dec., Tom Barns, dec., Clifford Trezise (Pendeen), dec., Charles Penrose, Phil Lang, dec., Bernard Blewett, Will Pearce, Vivian Philp, Stella Airey, Russell Philp, Hazel Jelbert, Roy Owens, Marjorie Stoddern.

My sincere thanks to Len Truran, his kind encouragement and guidance made this publication possible.

Not forgetting all the other wonderful friends from Hayle, who helped and prodded me, until the book was finished.
  I can only hope, I haven't disappointed them.

Des Philp

Preface

The little lad followed his mother's gaze across the road to Cannicott's grocery shop.

An old lady was slowly trudging along, without looking right or left. Under her arm she carried a small, battered, cardboard suitcase, held together by string.

"Where she go'n ma?" the lad asked.

"Madron Workhouse", the mother replied, "nine more miles to go".

When I first started to collect my notes some years ago, the old lady was the first to come to mind. I decided then to write about the real people as I knew them.

But with the pathos, and heartbreak, there was also much humour, and the book hasn't finally emerged as I had originally intended.

The stories are not in chronological order, and with few references to help me, I must for most part rely on my fading memory, with thankful hints from many good friends.

This is how we lived, how we laughed, how we struggled on from day to day, hoping for a better tomorrow.

> O What long sad years have gone,
> Since thy church was taught this prayer,
> O What eyes have watched and wept,
> For the dawning everywhere.
>   John Page Hopps. 1834–1912

Serita Philp – nee Whitford. My mother

Francis Leonard Philp. My father

1

The very early years

I was born on a cold winter's day, December 16th 1924. My parents had another son, but I was the younger by seven years.

My father Francis Leonard Philp, was a carpenter, and my mother's christian name was Serita, her only claim to doubtful fame, was, that as a young schoolgirl, the painter Henry Scott Tuke had chosen her as the subject of one of his paintings.

They must have been a very dispirited couple indeed, they had so longed for a little girl, and now the ultimate disappointment, another boy. I doubt if they ever forgave me.

And so I howled my way into the world at 22* St John's Street, Hayle, a small three roomed house, with only the one bedroom. My cot had seen better days, most probably father had had it given to him. He had cut away the mesh bottom, broken in so many places, and replaced it with wire-netting. I slept in this cot until I was five years old, the heavier I got, the more the netting stretched, until it finally resembled a hammock. But how snug and very comfortable it was.

It wasn't until I managed to stand upright, that I realised that something was very, very wrong. I didn't understand the meaning of poverty, but I seemed to be living in a void. There were no toys to play with, no books or pictures to look at. My world consisted of a tiny courtyard, with a water barrel in the corner.

I spent many hours standing on a stool, and staring into that barrel, watching the minnows my brother had caught and incarcerated in its depths, and the ever present little red worms, that seemed to be wriggling everywhere.

In retropsect, I believe that I can remember these very early days, only because life was so uneventful, and devoid of any interest, that

*Street numbers have since been changed.

1

even a tiny insignificant happening at that time, indelibly implanted itself on my memory.

There was, of course, the weekly excursion to my grandparents, on my mothers side, at Ventonleague, less than half a mile away. But it wasn't something I looked forward to.

With an astrakan bonnet pulled over my head, a handdown from my brother, I would be plonked into the push-chair, and whisked off to Ventonleague.

Oh, how I hated that chair.

A sombre, black iron and canvas affair, with a varnished wooden foot rest. Here was I, a big boy in my estimation, I could actually walk about, with admittably more confidence than my ability allowed, but nevertheless I was able to look after myself. Why couldn't I be left to my own devices and given the freedom that my new-found independence yearned for.

No way – I had to suffer the shame and degradation of being wheeled out in that infernal contraption, and what for?, to visit a bunch of silly simpering adults. I knew exactly what would happen. As soon as I tried to speak, they would double up with fits of laughing, while I stood frustrated, glaring at them with murder in my heart.

Grown-ups never seem to appreciate how much hate can generate in a small child. I think that must have been when I first developed a ferocious temper, and its a cross I've had to bear ever since.

But I had one trump card.

In their grown-up stupidity they reasoned that because I couldn't speak fluently, it naturally followed that I could not understand their spoken words.

How wrong they were.

At times the teen-age girls of the village gathered in Grandmother's shop, and discussed their latest love exploits in lurid and explicit detail. No one took any notice of the little ignorant toddler, playing in the corner, but I listened to all of it, understood some of it, and smiled inwardly at the thought of sharing their secrets.

But these very early memories are only fragmental glimpses of the past. The Trams at Camborne, a steam locomotive puffing leisurely across the level-crossing at Foundry swing bridge, and looking up at St Elwyn's church tower, expecting it to fall over at any minute. And then back again to my lonely little world of the courtyard.

I yearned for someone to talk to, why did my parents only speak to me in monosyllables, and why was I to be always condemned to wearing patched-up leave-offs? I was growing up fast, and learning what poverty was all about, and I soon realised that it was all my parents could do, to provide the necessities, there was little time or thought given to pampering young children.

When mother answered a knock at the front door, I would follow her and peer from behind her "Pinny" and out into the street. What a wonderful place it seemed to be.

It was fairly wide, but the surface of clay and stone had long since given away to neglect. On the opposite side there was still the remains of an old street gutter, after a heavy rain, the children sailed their little paper boats down this stream, to finally watch them tumble through the iron grid cover on Cornubia Hill.

There was no mains water supply in those early days, we carried our drinking water, by the bucketful, from the street pump outside St John's Church, at the junction to Cross Street. There was another pump at the other end of the street, near Copperhouse Chapel, both approximately equi-distant from our house, but we only used the St John's pump.

The council never maintained these relics of Victoriana, when they broke down, the neighbours shanghied father into making the necessary repairs. Usually the weighted clack-valve had disintegrated. A carefully shaped piece of shoe leather, with a brass bolt for a weight, soon remedied the situation. The water flowed and all were refreshed.

At night the street was plunged into almost total darkness, the only feeble illumination came from a single burner gaslight, throwing a circle of yellow around a cast-iron lamp-post just outside Jimmy Cox's house.

The middle classes turned up their noses and referred to us as the "White Apron Street". Why we should be singled out for this derogatory term is a bit of a mystery. It is true that the wives did tend to exchange the gossip of the day with each other, from their doorways, and all sported a bleached cotton pinny, or had utilised a "Spillers" flour bag for the same purpose.

But old photographs of other streets show similarily dressed women chatting to each other.

The intended slur was not deserved. The average family were just decent hard working folk, making the best of what little they had.

The rents in the street were very low, mother paid 1/6 a week for our three roomed home, any maintenance necessary was expected to be executed by the tenants themselves and many houses, although structurally sound, showed signs of serious neglect. The downstairs floors were simply made up of bricks embedded in a layer of sand. These floors played havoc with the cheap linoleum covering, straw and rag mats proved much more effective and lasting.

As I am writing, there is still one house in the street with a brick floor.

All the houses had long back gardens, and looking back I now believe that it was gardens that helped pull us through.

We couldn't afford seed potatoes, mother planted potato skins. Fertilized by liberal applications of horse manure, collected from the street, she would harvest quite a good crop, much to the astonishment of my father. The rest of the garden under his management didn't seem to do quite as well.

I seldom went into the garden, it was under constant cultivation, little boys were not encouraged to run amuck in that domain.

But I had to make the safari to the top of the garden when nature called. The lavatory was a wooden affair, with a bench type seat. The earthenware pan emptied itself into a hole in the ground just behind the structure. The hole was covered by some wooden planks, and seemed constantly on the verge of collapse. It could hardly be called a cesspit, although of course that was its function. The toilet was flushed twice a day with buckets of water drawn from the barrel in the courtyard, a rather burdensome task, just one of those things that everyone accepted, had to be done. I can't remember how we coped with the summer drought, but the mind boggles.

Alas there was something lurking in that garden, striking terror to my young heart.

His name was "Jasper".

Jasper was a gargantuan rooster of doubtful parentage, a vicious beast with long spurs and a glittering eye. He was the undisputed king of our vegetable patch. Cats and dogs fled in dismay at his approach. He seemed to have an intense hatred for everything that moved. He attacked my mother many times, but a well-aimed blow with a broom drove him back in frustrated fury. He filled me with apprehension and I knew he had already marked me as an easy prey.

It was the same caper each day, I would creep stealthily up the path, hoping the beast hadn't seen me, but he always did. I reached the safety of the lav' in the nick of time, with the feathered fiend close on my heels. I slammed the door shut and shot the bolt, at least I was safe for a little while. But by this time Jasper had already reasoned in his evil little brain, that I was in there and soon would have to come out again, and he strutted around the hut triumphantly proclaiming in a loud voice, his pending victory, and leaving me in no doubt what would happen when I again ventured outside.

There was only one thing to do. Yell loud and long, until someone from the house heard me, came to my rescue, and escorted me back down the path.

My parents thought the business with the rooster was a collosal joke, they never seemed to understand how fearful such a confrontation can be to a young child.

– Until one day –

Jasper had developed a new tactic. He pretended not to see me, and looking in the opposite direction he appeared to be contentedly picking at the ground, but at the same time edging slowly backwards. Before I could break into my sprint, he displayed his battle colours, in a panic I tripped and fell full-length to the ground. Without hesitation the feathered fiend closed on me, ripping his spur through the calf of my leg.

Father hearing my screams, raced to the rescue. Jasper had already run for cover. I was picked up and carried back to the house. Mother bathed and bandaged my leg, and did her best to comfort me. She turned to father,

"This isn't funny any more Leonard".

He didn't say anything, just walked across to his tool-bag, lying in the corner of the kitchen, and took out the razor sharp carpenters axe. Opening the back door, he walked across the courtyard, up the steps, and into the garden.

The next day a very different looking Jasper, featherless, and headless, graced our dinner table.

And I ate him with relish.

I was at long last being allowed into the street, but for brief periods only. All the other children seemed much older, and I reasoned that some kind of peace offering as an introduction, might be a good way of currying favour.

Some days before, I had found an old discarded child's pedal cycle, in the brambles of the garden.

I pulled it free, and inspected my new found acquisition. The wooden forks, handle bars, and seat, were in the last stages of decay, and the

St John's Street (circa 1900). No. 22, far right, dark facade.
(photo: K. Harris)

St John's Street. 1991. No. 22 now with white facade

pedals had long since parted company with the rusty front wheel.

It was the first toy I ever had, and although I could do little more than sit on it, in my imagination I travelled far and wide on that gleaming "Douglas".

This then would be my contribution, my passport of acceptance to the boys and girls of the street. I carried it through the house, and parked it just under the frontroom window. Within minutes it had been commandeered and whisked away. To my consternation I saw quite large boys treating my offering as a pathetic joke.

Up and down they pushed each other, shrieking with laughter, Until finally my proud possession disintegrated before my eyes. The loss of the cycle, and worse, my total rejection, reduced me to tears, but there was no sympathy from my mother. "It's your own fault", she said, "You shouldn't have taken it out there". Although I had a feeling that she was really glad to be rid of something, that she had always regarded as, "a piece of untidy rubbish".

I was beginning to realise, that the world outside my courtyard, was perhaps after all, not the wonderful adventureland I had imagined it to be.

I was now old enough to accompany my parents on their evening walks, and happily without the assistance of that push-chair monstrosity.

We were returning from Phillack one evening, when my father spotted a man wearing a rather dilapitated raincoat, standing at the edge of the old Copperhouse dry dock. He was staring as if transfixed, at something in the water. I almost choked with horror as I saw the object of his attention.

A Spaniel dog, a dog with a large stone tied around its neck. Instead of sinking to the bottom, and quickly drowning, the dog had found the strength to keep afloat, and miraculously was holding its head just clear of the water. Panic stricken, it was swimming 'round and 'round in circles, looking for a way to save itself, but with the surface of the water many feet from the top of the quay, there was no way out.

Still 'round and 'round, slower and slower it swam, with the man in the raincoat passively standing on the dock edge. "You callous s – , shouted father, "Why didn't you borrow a gun, and shoot it". The man didn't turn or answer, just stood there, watched and waited. Mother hurried me away, "Hardly the sort of thing a child should see", she said.

That night, lying in bed, I could still see the silent man. I could still see the brown and white Spaniel fighting for its life, with a stone tied to its neck. And I remember most of all, its eyes, pleading eyes, glazed with hopelessness.

That night I prayed my first prayer. I don't know what I expected, Possibly some vision of divine intervention, someone, anyone, to go down to the dock, and rescue the animal. I had never been taught to pray, no doubt, as usual, I had jumbled every thing up, and made a hash of it. After a time I realised that all was not well, no one had heard me.

"O Lord, how long shall I cry,
and thou wilt not hear.
Habakkuk. C.1. V.2.

It was a very troubled little boy, that finally fell asleep that night.

My push-chair seemed to have somehow disappeared, probably passed on to some other unfortunate. What happened to it, I never knew, and I never asked.

It was the end of the Very Early Days.

2

A time for learning

The older I got, the less frequent the walks with my parents. But on these now rare occasions, father did try to make things a little more interesting, with his potted histories.

Walking along the quay, he would stop and say, "This is where they had the'Iron Grid'. Old railway lines had been utilised to make a sloping grid. Ships would be pulled out of the water on to the rails, and then laid over on their side. This was called, careening. In this position, repairs to the bottom and keel of the vessel were much easier facilitated. The Swan Pool at Foundry was one of my parent's favourite walks.

"See that wall", he pointed to the broken wall on the far side of the pool.

"They made hawsers behind that wall, it was a roofed workshop in the old days, we called it the 'Rope Walk', the rope winding occupied the whole length of that building".

The first cottage on Foundry Hill seemed to interest him.

"Look there", strung on wires around the facia board, a row of glass bottle necks. Obviously at one time they had been a crude form of ariel insulator.

I had heard the story many times. Just after the turn of the century, an amateur wireless pioneer lived in the house, he built a transmitter and receiver, and successfully sent morse code messages which were picked up, two miles away near Lelant.

In 1901, Guglielmo Marconi astounded the world, when he flashed a signal from Poldhu near the Lizard, across the Atlantic to Newfoundland.

Marconi heard about the Cornishman, invited him to Poldhu, and they spent a very entertaining day together.

Who was the Cornishman? I doubt if anyone alive today will remember. My father knew his name, but he is no longer here to tell us.

The Copperhouse docks, the Black Road, and Black Arch, were all built from black slag blocks. The slag scraped from the top of the molten copper, and poured into moulds. Today they are still in situ, after 200 years, virtually indestructable.

It was on the Black Road, that we met our local chemist, Ernest Frederick Uren, known to us all as Ernie.

Ernie was a fund of stories, his ancestry steeped in local history. His story of the Rector's (or Priest's) Arch, lost nothing in the telling.

Black Arch, some call it Black Bridge, had a peculiarity. It consisted of two arches, one much higher than the other, the higher one was called, Rector's or Priest's Arch. The Black Road was built as an easy access from the Copper Works to the docks. It also squared off the end of Copperhouse Reach, leaving the creek to languish into obscurity.

A bridge was built to accommodate the river that wound its way through the creek, and a design of two arches was decided upon.

But alas, in the words of the great Bard, "there was a rift in the lute".

The rector of Phillack, Reverend William Hocken, had a personal interest in the bridge building venture. His beloved sailing boat was moored in the creek, alongside the Glebe, and with the two arches now half completed, he suddenly realised that his pride – and – joy was effectively land-locked.

The Rector was, without doubt, the most powerful man in the Parish. When he waxed wrathful, and shouted "Stop", they stopped, the great Cornish Copper Company blanched, when they heard those stentorian tones. A meeting was hurriedly called by the Company, in a vain hope to reach some mutual agreement. William was adamant, his access to the sea inviolable, the bridge must be altered to suit.

Tearfully the Company ordered one arch to be demolished, and rebuilt much higher.

The Rector viewed the completed bridge with satisfaction. At high water, his craft safely negotiated under the higher arch, hoisted mast and canvas, and sailed happily into the sunset.

The Riviere House was built some 200 years ago, and stands on the Northern slopes of Copperhouse Reach. This slate covered edifice, commands a panoramic view of the town, and the waterway. Probably the best sited property in the district. It should be, it was originally a residence for one of the hierarchy of the Cornish Copper Company.

Like all houses of elegance, it had its ghost, (don't they all)? A lady working in service, reported seeing a carriage-and-pair come noiselessly up the drive, and suddenly disappear. Whatever the manifestation, it seems to have given up its nocturnal haunting habits. During my lifetime, I have never heard of a re-occurrence of this ghostly phenomenon.

Before the First World War, Virginia Bateman lived there, with her son Compton Mackenzie, and her young daughter Fay. Fay Compton was described as "solid and sedate". Sedate maybe, but my father remembered her as anything but solid, admittably his brief sighting would have been a few years later.

As a young lad he was sent to the house to deliver a letter. A servant asked him to wait in the hall, presumably for a reply and hopefully a tip. It was then he saw Fay Compton for the first and only time.

She came out of an upstairs room, leaned on the hand-rail, and looked down at him.

Father described her as a pale faced, very frail young lady. "I had a feeling", he said, "That a puff of wind would blow her away". The servant returned to tell him there was no reply. The proffered generous tip, was thankfully received.

Then there was the Smugglers Cave, few writers bother to mention it in their knowledgeable tomes of local history. My parents dismissed the legend as rubbish, and Ethel E. Bicknell, in her holiday guide, "Hayle and Phillack" published by, The Homeland Assoc' Ltd, circa 1911, expressed a doubt, when she wrote about the Black Cliffs and caves.

"One of these caves extends under the shifting sand,
so local tradition says, to Riviere House!
(The italic is mine.)

It was in the early 1940's, that a friend suggested that we make an investigation to try and solve the enigma.

The house had been empty for some time, to gain access to the grounds, all one had to do, was open the gate. Alas the garden was enveloped in brambles, and without proper tools we decided to give up the venture.

Then through the growth we saw it, just a few yards from the side of the house. The tunnel had been driven into the rising ground, with the aid of a miner's carbide lamp, we started the investigation.

What surprised us at first, was the fact that the tunnel we entered had been lined with stone, and not just cut into the rock, as was expected. Suddenly, after a short distance, we came to an obstruction, the tunnel had been sealed off by a stone wall. However all was not lost, for in the middle of the wall there was an opening of less than 2 feet square. Crawling through this aperture, we found ourselves in a cave of clay and loose stones. A few yards further on it came to an abrupt end, the holes of the miners picks were still in evidence. There were no side tunnels, and it was obvious what had happened.

The cave was simply intended as an adit, a water drain outlet, from the Wheal Lucy mine on Hayle Towans. After driving the adit for only a short distance, and finding themselves working in soft loose stone and clay, the project was deemed unsuitable, and abandoned.

But I suppose the smugglers cave story will forever be recounted. In recent years, excited children from our local schools, have been shown the entrance of this fascinating piece of local history.

Sorry, boys and girls, it's just a story from someone's fertile imagination.

But don't tell the tourists, they love these bits of nonsense.

3

Boy in the chair

I was still too young to be left alone in the house, for any length of time. Wherever my mother went, I had to be dragged along also.

Mrs Evans lived in a house on the corner of St John's Street, and Cornubia Hill, just opposite Sam Blewett's shop. About once a week mother would call on her, and together they exchanged the local gossip. I was despatched into the courtyard, to talk to Johnny. He was a lad about 14 years of age, he sat in an old deckchair, in the sunshine of the courtyard. Deep set eyes stared from an anguished face, as if he was trying to say, "Help me, please help me". His boots were only half laced, he hadn't the strength to tie them properly, and every few minutes he coughed into an earthenware jar, and then wipe his lips, with a red stained handkerchief.

We never spoke to each other, and although no one bothered to tell me, I knew that Johnny was dying of consumption. (We learned about these things, at a very early age in the street). So I just stood and watched him, as he slowly deteriorated before my eyes. I was considered far too young to comprehend exactly what the situation was, but I pieced the jig-saw together in my own way. It was useless trying to get information from my parents, such things were never discussed with children, but overheard, whispered conversations, had given me a fair idea.

I knew the situation had finally, and sadly, resolved itself, when one morning mother donned a black coat, and father came down the stairs in his blue-serge suit, purchased a few months before, from "Sangwin's", gents outfitters on Fore St, and reserved only for special occasions. Nobody needed to tell me what this special occasion was.

I was to be left alone for an hour, and tersely told to behave myself, – or else – .

Some minutes later, perched in the bedroom window, I peered 'round the paper roll-up blind, and up the street. A horse-drawn hearse was slowly pulling away from the Evans' house.

13

Boy in the chair

I knew I would never see Johnny again.

Many times, over the years, I have often thought about him, and collecting notes for this book, I made enquiries from a few who had lived in the street in those far-off days. But none seemed to remember, the "Boy in the Chair".

Perhaps it was just a figment of childhood imagination, a dream, or a story I had heard from somewhere and distorted. Just as I had given up, Three people, Edna Wearne, Willie Hammond, and Bernard Blewett, whose parents ran the shop opposite the Evan's house, recalled the lad to memory.

Looking through some old photos of my mother's, I came across a snapshot of a young lad, sitting in a deckchair in a courtyard. His boots half laced, his face unsmiling, his eyes still pleading, just within reach, the chemical mask to ease the breathing, and near his foot, that awful earthenware jar.

> "Can I but dream; as I lie still,
> In the cold, cold, sands of Phillack Hill,
> Someone might see my marker there,
> And remember me; in silent prayer".
>
> D.P.

Rest in peace Johnny, we haven't all forgotten.

4

Sunday school

My first scholastic experience was the Sunday school. It was an unwritten law that little children were not allowed to play, outside the house, on the Lord's day. It wasn't the nice thing to do, although my mother thought the self-imposed restriction rather ridiculous. Nevertheless she fell in line with her neighbours. Alas, a child running amuck in a house of only three rooms, did nothing for domestic peace and serenity. There was the only one solution, the Sunday school, at least it would afford an hour or more respite.

The Parish Church had re-opened the St John's Street Mission as a Sunday school, under the kindly guidance of Mrs Biggleston. Although we were, "not of the elite" a suit of fairly respectable clothes was always kept in a drawer, for Sundays, and Sundays only. So with my shoes polished, and sporting a clean shirt, (luxury indeed) I toddled off to my first ever religious instruction. The street pump perched outside the Mission gate, offered a challenge, but as always I found the handle too resistant for my feeble efforts.

The Sunday school boasted only about ten pupils, but just being there, was a wonderful experience for me. The other children were all strangers, I think they came from another planet, they were all so quiet and well behaved, it was unbelievable. I listened intently to the biblical stories, and sang the hymns with squeaky, off-key gusto. I could read a few words, but I learned the first verse of "Now the day is over", parrot-fashion, and nobody seemed to mind when I sang the same words to all the other verses.

But it was to be a short lived experience, just before Christmas the pupils were going to be transferred to the Parish Church at Phillack, a distance of more than a mile, and much too far for me. Mrs Biggleston realised that some of us, unable to effect the transition, would not qualify for the annual prize. She decided to arrange a Christmas present for us, of our own choice. When she asked me what present I would like, I

16

surprised her, by saying, "A book, a book of pictures and stories". An odd request from someone who could hardly read at all.

"Why", she asked, "do you want such a present"?

I replied without hesitation, "Because I've never had a book of my own, and I want to read".

On the following Sunday, Mrs Biggleston presented me with my book, "Little Dots Annual", I couldn't believe it, full of drawings, photos, poems, and stories, all beautifully presented on good quality paper. It had cost 3/6, in my small world an unbelievable sum to spend on a book.

All good things must come to an end, and it was time to say goodbye to the Mission.

With my halcyon Sunday school days now in limbo, I again drove my mother to distraction on the Lord's day. Reluctantly she decided to send me to the Chapel, at the other end of the street. A decision born from desperation, as my parents had always viewed with suspicion, the many business interests that sang so lustily within its hallowed walls.

Copperhouse Chapel, was a complex of three buildings, built at varying times over many years. There was the Sunday school, the oldest building, at one time a day school, then the centre building, which housed a library of countless books, and finally the large Chapel itself, towering over all.

I arrived at the complex, not quite knowing what to expect. How many children attended, I do not know, it could have been 200, or even more. After assembly we had the opening prayer and then a hymn. It was now the children broke away into their respective classes. Bedlam erupted, the older children raged through the three buildings like Banshees, with the teachers frantically running about, in an endeavour to round up the rebels, but to little avail. Eventually classes, much depleted, were assembled, and the hard pressed, set about trying to drum some religious instruction into little deaf ears.

Books had always fascinated me, probably because I only had the one. I made enquiries about the Chapel library, only to be told that these books were only for grown-ups, and then only for those who were Chapel "members". I slowly began to realise, that in fact, there were two grades of worshippers, the "members" who were the elite, and people like myself, who were tolerated only to make up the numbers.

It soon became painfully obvious that my timing did not meet with general approval. The other children, and even the teachers themselves,

17

pointed out that the annual awards were only two weeks away, in no way would I qualify for a coveted prize. I tried to explain that I knew nothing about prizes, but no one listened. I was silently labelled, a crafty interloper, the Chapel had long experience with such nasties, and I was certainly not going to reap the benefit from this, all too obvious, subterfuge.

The great day arrived, and we shuffled into the Chapel, all spotlessly turned out, and for once, on our best behaviour. At last I was to see what all the fuss was about.

I couldn't believe my eyes, it was like an Aladdin's cave. A continuation of tables stretched across the front of the Rostrum, piled high, from end to end, with all kinds of books. It was usual in those days, to bulk purchase, over-print books, at a fraction of their recommended price. Nothing wrong with that, they were of course, all brand new.

I watched the proceedings with interest. The lady doling out the prizes, wheezed a few words of congratulation to the recipients, and everyone, not hearing a word she said, clapped dutifully. A few of the children had really fine books, like the splendid, "Treasury of English Literature", or "Greyfriars Holiday Annual", no over-prints here. For the few fully dedicated, who also attended the morning service, there was an extra presentation of a Bible, or a Hymn book. I quickly summed up the situation. The Bible and Hymn book were out, I would never attend the morning service anyway. But that "Treasury" or "Greyfriars", could be mine, if I put in a really good attendance, over the next twelve months.

And so it was to be. Every Sunday afternoon, I walked to the Sunday School and suffered more than an hour of sheer boredom. Nothing would stop me this time, and I eagerly looked forward to the day, when I would walk proudly home, with the magnificent tome tucked under my arm.

A year later, I sat again in the Chapel, and watched the procession of children to the front. My book was there, somewhere at the end of the table. I had only missed two classes through illness, but had been informed that sickness was not a discredit to the overall marking.

At last the lady with the soft, rather affected voice, read out my name, and picked up a very slender volume, with glazed card covers, the sort of thing that could have been bought for about fourpence, but as an over-print, probably cost less than half that price. I walked to the table in a daze, I wanted to shout, "You idiot, you've got it wrong, my book is one of those at the end of the table, the big ones".

"King Barbine", she beamed, and handed me the epistle, amid a little half-hearted applause. I returned crestfallen to the pew. What had gone wrong? I had a good marking, but somehow I had missed the boat.

I walked home that day in some trepidation, trying to comfort myself, that at least it was something to read, but knowing that I still had to face the wrath of the family.

As I feared, the family erupted in fury, "King Barbine" was flung across the room, the accompanying expletives are best left unwritten.

There was a simple explanation. The large expensive books were only awarded to children whose parents had subscribed an extra penny or two each week, to a prize fund, this was in addition to the usual collection. The more they gave, the better the prize. I suppose it was another way of separating the "haves" from the "have-nots".

The fact that I attended the Sunday school for all the wrong reasons, never occurred to me, I was embittered, and shocked into delusion. I never again regularly attended a Sunday school, until the Salvation Army opened their new citadel on Cross Street, in 1936.

I thought I had washed my hands of the Chapel, but in another chapter, you'll read, that a Methodist from that same Chapel came into our lives, with compassion and charity, when we needed it the most.

"King Barbine", soon fell to pieces, and, I suppose, found its way into the fire-grate.

It was much later that I learned, that Mrs Biggleston's present, was a personal gift. The Church had made no contribution to it. The "Little Dots Annual", is still on my bookshelf. My mother told me that I must always keep it, in remembrance of a very kind lady. So that I wouldn't forget, she wrote inside the cover;

"From Mrs Bicklestone, Clifton Terrace, Hayle".
– Spelling was never my mother's forte –

5

The painting

My mother often told me of the time, she posed for the famous painter, Henry Scott Tuke.

As a schoolgirl Serita Whitford boasted incredibly long hair, so long in fact, that she could actually sit on it.

One day, Tuke was driving his pony and jingle through Hayle, when he spotted her. The artist with the piercing eyes frightened her so much, that when he attempted to talk to her, she simply ran away. Undaunted, he followed the girl to her home, the grocery shop on Beatrice Terrace.

He introduced himself to the family, and expressed a desire to paint a portrait of the girl, explaining that he had taken a house at Lelant for a short period. He requested that Serita be brought there each Sunday, until the painting was finished. Not only would he use her as a model, but actually pay for the privilege.

And so it came about. On Sunday mornings, my grandfather and his little daughter walked down to the harbour, took the row-boat ferry across the river, and then strolled on to the Tuke residence in Lelant, a total distance of about 2½ miles. She spent most of the day there, to be collected again by her father, at 4pm, and escorted home.

My mother never had a holiday in the whole of her life, but she often referred to the times she spent at Lelant, as the happiest, "It was", she said, "like living in another world". She posed very little, Not more than a couple of spells of about 20 minutes in the day. The rest of the time she spent happily with the cook or the gardener, they seemed to have made quite a fuss of her. Tuke gave her an old violin to play with, which she carried around, and strummed, with little musical expertise.

There was a lady living with Tuke, and the little girl naturally assumed that this was his wife, and always referred to her as such. (actually it was his sister, herself a very fine painter) But it never occurred to Serita, that these kind and talented people, could, and did, suffer tantrums, and suddenly fly-off-the-handle.

Maria Tuke had been for some time, engrossed in a painting on wood. At last it was finished, she burst in on her unsuspecting brother.

"There it is, now what do you think about it?"

Henry Scott peered over the top of his easel.

"Ah – er – yes, very good, very good indeed", he conceded.

"Do you really think so", she looked at him suspiciously.

"Yes I do", he confirmed, it is very good.

"Well I damn well don't think so", she turned on her heel, strode out into the garden, snatched up the wood-cutters axe, and chopped the offending masterpiece into small pieces.

The girl spectator couldn't understand what all the fuss was about. After all, if the picture hadn't come up to scratch, why not just give it to her, she would have treasured it as a momento, of her happy days at the big house. But artists tend to live in a little world of their own, the painting was destined for destruction, the whim of a little child hardly warranted consideration.

Finally the painting of Serita was finished. She had often looked at it in its various stages, and described herself as wearing a green dress, with one arm bare. Her father collected her for the last time, and asked Tuke if he could see the finished canvas. But the painter refused, no outsider was to look at it until it was hung in the forth-coming exhibition.

More than a little disgruntled, the father and daughter returned to Hayle.

The story might easily have finished there, but some years later, during the First World War, – an odd occurrence –

Serita, now in her twenties, and not yet married, was still living with her parents, at Beatrice Terrace.

The wounded from the fields of Flanders, had filled the hospitals to overflowing, and convalescing soldiers were billeted out into private homes. Two were billeted with the Whitfords.

At meal times, one of the soldiers seemed to keep looking at her, with a strange curiosity. One morning he suddenly exclaimed, "I've got it, you've been painted, but it's some years ago". She briefly told him about Tuke, and the happy times she spent at Lelant, while still a schoolgirl.

"I knew", he continued, "I had seen you somewhere before, it was while I was in hospital, I saw a reproduction of the painting in an illustrated magazine". It looked as if Tuke had in fact had the painting hung.

Serita married a local carpenter, Francis Leonard Philp, in 1916, although he had been a member of the Territorials, he was declared unfit for the Regular Army.

They often talked about Tuke, and Leonard reasoned that if the painting had been hung, and a magazine had seen fit to reproduce it, somewhere there must be a photograph or a print available. They decided to do a little detecting.

The lady at Lelant Post Office informed them that the artist only resided in the village for a short time, and had moved on many years before. However the Housekeeper was still alive, and living in retirement, in the village. She gave them directions to find the cottage.

An old lady answered the cottage door. Yes she remembered the little girl very well indeed, and invited them inside. Over tea, they chatted merrily away about the Tukes and the painting. It appeared, the artist resided at Lelant, for a short period only, probably renting the large house and its servants, from a friend. But the old lady had no idea what had happened to them. However she recalled that Tuke and Stanhope Forbes were good friends, and suggested that a visit to Forbes at Newlyn might bear fruit.

Later that day they were standing outside the palatial Forbes residence at Newlyn. A servant girl, in white lace and black alpaca took the proffered questionaire, closed the door, and left them waiting in expectation, on the door-step.

A few minutes later she returned. "Mr Forbes did not wish to see them, he knew nothing of anyone called Tuke, and had no idea where such a person might be."

And so the investigation fell on stoney ground.

There is no doubt that the two artists were good friends, this has been documented in photographs, and Forbes is known to have considered Tuke a very fine painter indeed.

Forbes was often seen sketching around Hayle at that time, but my father's courteous salutations to the great man, had given way to a basilisk stare.

Tuke's paintings today, are much sought after by collectors, and every few years, exhibitions of his work are featured at the Cornish towns of Falmouth and Penzance.

The art critics, and collectors, seem very reluctant to admit, that an unlisted "Tuke" exists somewhere. One informed me, that Tuke never resided at Lelant, and yet there is a book in the local library, with a chapter on the artist, with the village of Lelant mentioned only in passing, but no details.

In a 1986 art catalogue, a Tuke painting was offered for sale, "Cornish Girl. 1909." This was advertised as the only painting of a young Cornish girl, by this artist.

The picture reproduced in the catalogue, certainly wasn't my mother, she would have been 20 years old at that time.

The art world is at last taking notice, somewhere, someday, they'll discover the lost painting, the portrait of a little girl, with exceptionally long hair.

I wonder, if ever, I shall see it?

6

O God take me home

She lived much further along the street, and I often wondered if she was a witch. To a young child she certainly looked like one, and didn't I see a Besom in her courtyard, what more proof was required.

Of course it was just a childhood fantasy, like many working class wives, she had aged before her time. The struggle to bring up a large family, on a mere pittance, had taken its toll. To me she looked very, very, old, but in retrospect, she couldn't have been more than in her mid 50's, her youngest child was barely 14.

I remember her, as a small woman, dressed in Edwardian black, with stud fastening boots. Her hair hung dark and lank, a sharp long nose protruded from a sallow face. When she spoke, each rasped word, penetrated the ear drum like a pistol shot. She scurried here and there, like a frightened animal, and unknowingly, scared the living daylights out of me.

Every night about 7pm, she peered around her front door, and after satisfying herself that the coast was clear, whipped out of the house, and down the hill. At the "Cornubia" she purchased a bottle of "Guinness", from the ladies bar, little more than a cubby-hole at the rear of the premises. (Female participants of the demon drink, were not given much encouragement at that establishment). With her treasured acquisition hidden from all prying eyes, under her pinny, she returned to her sanctum in the street. Behind closed, locked doors, and drawn curtains, she sat in front of the Slab, and happily imbibed in the dark nectar, oblivious to the fact that the whole street knew exactly what she was doing, and having a good laugh at her expense.

Today the exercise would seem superficial, to say the least, but more than 60 years ago, with the working classes, the codes of conduct were very narrow indeed.

When the lady became terminally ill, word soon echoed through the street – Cancer – During the last agonising days, she was watched over

24

by her young son, who had to forego his schooling, to be at her side. He knew the writing was on the wall, when the doctor handed him a bottle of medicine, which was simply a mixture of morphine and alchohol. The instructions were explicit, one teaspoonful, every four hours, day and night, but under no circumstance must the doseage be increased. And so every four hours, the boy gave his mother the prescribed teaspoonful.

But after only a few days, the effect of the drug was wearing off more quickly than anyone allowed for. For two hours she would be at peace with the world, then for the next two hours cry out in agony, "O God, take me home".

I heard the cries only once, when I passed the house with the half drawn curtains. "What's wrong with 'er ma", I asked. Mother dismissed my enquiry with curt impatience. "Don't take any notice, she's only a bit 'doo-ally'. But she fooled nobody, least of all me.

The end came very quickly, the young lad burst through our front door, and sat on a chair in the kitchen, with his head in his hands. Between sobs, he said, "She's gone". Mother proffered a cup of tea, and tried to console him. "It couldn't go on like that son, she's in a much better place now, no more pain, no more crying".

But the lad was inconsolable. He looked at my mother and said, "You don't understand, I couldn't sit there, day and night, listening to her cries, and doing nothing". Mother paled, she already knew the answer when she asked.

"What have you done boy?"

"I had to do it", he said, "O God I had to do it, I gave her the whole bottle, they're sure to find out, what will happen now?"

Mother quickly pulled herself together, "We'll stand by you and speak for you, but I don't know what will become of it, let's take one step at a time, first of all I'll notify the doctor".

The three of them met in the shaded bedroom. The old doctor adjusted his pince-nez, and examined the corpse.

"Of course, we were expecting it", he murmured. He wrote out the death certificate and handed it to the boy. "Keep this in a safe place, the undertaker will ask for it".

Mother and the lad watched without saying a word, perhaps all would be well after all, the doctor was already preparing to leave the bedroom. At the top of the stairs he paused, they followed his gaze across the room to the empty bottle on the marble-top washstand. He walked to the washstand and picked up the conspiratorial evidence, looked at them and said, "I think I'll get rid of this".

They followed him down the winding staircase, and out into the courtyard. Without ceremony he dropped the bottle into the rusty bucket used as a dust-bin. Adjusting his overcoat he looked up at the scudding rainclouds, with a hint of blue trying to break through.

"You know", he spoke very quietly, "I think it's going to be a nice day after all".

7

Mary Wall

Occasionally, my parents attended Sunday service at Phillack Church, and it was the Vicar from that ancient pile, who approached them with a problem and a proposition. There was an old lady living in a two-roomed cottage at Ventonleague, by the name of Mary Wall. She was fiercely independent, not very approachable, and appeared to be suffering from dementia, (today her condition would be diagnosed as Alzheimer's disease) The Church had tried to keep an eye on her, and decided, it would be in her best interest, if someone could call on her once a day, give the house a quick clean-through, but above all, make certain that Mary was buying sufficient food for herself, and once a week insist she take a bath. About an hour each day should suffice. It did mean that mother would have to walk more than half a mile to the village, every day, and seven days a week. For this service to humanity, the Church would pay her, from its Parish funds, the princely sum of two-shillings per week, considered the going rate at that time. Well the money, little as it was, would certainly come in handy, and mother became, what today we would call, a home help.

The scene of neglect, when she opened the door on that first day, was indescribable. Everything edible seemed to be in the last throes of putrefaction, the last meal that Mary had eaten was a few bites at a part loaf of bread, green with mould. "Before we do any cleaning", mother said, "The first and most important priority, is getting you some decent food".

" 'avn't no money", spat out the old woman.

"Let's see", returned mother, grabbing Mary's hand-bag and tipping out the contents. A grubby handkerchief, comb, small scissors, a few pennies, and two pieces of folded brown-coloured paper.

"You have two ten-shilling notes here, your pension for two weeks, and you haven't spent any of it".

"That's mine", screamed the old woman, "Put it down or I'll – ".

From under her pinny she suddenly produced a pointed kitchen knife. Mother grabbed her wrist, and wrestled the weapon from her grasp. She now realised one very important thing. Facing Mary Wall, these situations could be handled fairly easily, because the old woman was very frail, but on no account must one ever turn the back on her.

Armed with one of the ten-shilling notes, mother walked to Penberthy's shop at the top of the hill, and purchased the necessary items. Returning to the cottage, she found Mary in a more placid mood, and the old lady was soon tucking into the first decent meal she had had for some time.

The once-a-week bath was a bit of a struggle, Mary protested and fought until her strength ebbed away, but finally gave in to the inevitable. It was the final blow of her independence, stripped, and forced to sit in a galvanised tub, while this interfering outsider, scrubbed her clean. The shame must have been unbearable.

And so it went on for about six months. Many times mother would come home, feeling absolutely fed up, and sickened by the whole business. If she didn't do it, Mary would have probably been incarcerated in a work-house, or, even more likely, succumbed to self-neglect. Every other day Mother vowed never to go again, but somehow managed to carry on, until Mary Wall finally passed away.

There was a cousin living up-country, and when this lady was informed, she hastily took a train to Hayle and made the necessary funeral arrangements. Mother was given a few pounds from the estate, in token of her sufference, a welcome addition indeed to our sparse funds. She was also told to take any odd'ments lying about, if she fancied them. So mother collected a few small pieces of pottery and glass-ware, two large silk handkerchiefs with a photograph developed in the centre, and Mary's Bible. But mother never had much consideration for bric-a-brac, and during the next few months the "unwanted" spent most of its time in our bucket dust-bin, only to be rescued, time and time again, by my father, loudly protesting, "What are you doing woman? these are worth a fortune".

During one of his numerous sojourns on the dole, father decided the time was ripe to reap the benefit of the legacy. The nearest antique shop was five miles away at St Ives. He carefully wrapped one of the pieces in newspaper, hopped on his trusty bicycle, and pedalled furiously away to seek his fortune.

The antique dealer was certainly interested, one of the pieces, a small vase, appeared to be of an opaque glass, and of some considerable value. He took my father's name and address, promising to call at St John's Street, later in the day, and give a valuation on the small collection.

A very happy man indeed cycled the five miles back to Hayle, he had been on the dole for the last two weeks, and money was in short supply. The dealer had hinted that the collection might be worth five pounds or even more, and Francis Leonard had visions of the ever worrying financial problem, being eased for many weeks to come.

He wheeled the cycle through the front door, and stood it against the staircase in the narrow passage. Mother came out of the kitchen in a surprisingly happy frame of mind. Before father could speak, she said. "I've got some good news Leonard, a chap's been here from St Ives, and bought Mary Wall's rubbish, gave me fifteen shillings, pity you took the vase with you, I could have sold that as well".

It was obvious what had happened, the dealer had jumped into his car and driven as fast as he could to Hayle, overtaking the cyclist on the way. Catching mother unawares, he proceeded to clinch the deal, much to his own greedy advantage. In his hurry he missed another item, and didn't seem interested in Mary's bible.

Utterly crestfallen, father sat at the kitchen table, there was nothing he could do but accept the situation. "That was a damn dirty trick", he turned to me, "You'll find boy, that in this life, when you're really down and out, there is always some s – , better off than you, just waiting, to kick you in the 'chaks'".

Over the years, the reamaining piece suffered breakage, and was thrown away.

I still have the old lady's Bible, a small leather bound New Testament, the front cover embossed;

Sold Under Cost Price.
British And Foreign Bible Society. Fourpence.

On the Flyleaf inscribed in copperplate handwriting;

Mary Wall. Borne 1848.
Mary Wall her book. A reward from Guildford Wesleyan Sundays School. B.P.B.B.

The little book was published in 1861.

Guildford is a cluster of houses on the outer edge of town, dominated by a granite railway viaduct. I have contacted the local Chapel historians, but none have any reference to a Chapel or a Sunday School at Guildford. Like Mary it has long since gone, and until now – forgotten –

8

Passing thro'

St John's Street seemed to have been a magnet for the street buskers, tinkers, and vagrants.

The gypsy, Mrs Burr, walked all the way from St Hilary, a distance of eight miles, to sell her clothes pegs in the back streets of Hayle, with her little daughter, Mary, strapped to her back. She was always thankful for the cup of tea and a bun, that mother gave her. Some years later when Mary had reached her teens, they bought themselves a pony and trap, which the young girl drove with in-born expertise.

All the gypsies I ever knew, seemed to be called "Burr", with the different families settling at St Hillary, Leedstown, and Chenhalls, (near St Erth). The Burr's at Chenhalls had their encampment on some waste ground, just below my Uncle Will's long garden. He referred to them as the "nicest of neighbours", interfered with no-one, and quietly kept their own counsel.

It was fascinating watching them make clothes pegs. Cutting Sycamore branches to size, with a sharp knife, splitting them about Two-thirds of the way, then plunging the stick into a can of bubbling water, boiling on an open fire. With the wood now in a ductile state, the split was opened to form a mouth, by forcing it over an axe head, held between the knees. A band of metal, cut with scissors from a cocoa tin, was wrapped around the peg, just above the split, and kept in place by a brass sprig. The whole operation was so fast it was unbelievable, about one minute per peg, would be an educated guess.

Many of the crippled from the Great War, had been reduced to beggary, hardly a just reward for services to their country, but these unfortunates were a common sight, around the back streets of Hayle.

There was a one-arm man who had been wounded in the hand, it was such a mess that the army surgeons would have preferred to amputate the whole arm, but the powers-that-be decreed that only the absolute minimum of surgery was to be carried out. He suffered four

31

operations as the infection spread, until the whole limb was finally removed.

"Take a look at him boy", my father said, "They tortured him just to try and save a few bob on his pension".

I was a little young to know who "they" were, it was a lesson I was to learn at a much later date.

Mr Munsen, a retired tea taster, still dabbled in his old trade, blending tea in his kitchen. He was a tall man, dressed immaculately in a dark suit, and his bearing was such, that he could wear the already dated butterfly collar, with some dignity. His tea was said to be exceptionally good, but I don't think we bought any, it was a little too expensive.

Mr Trythall walked through, selling various items of clothing from a suitcase, usually stopping at Lizzie Warren's for a little refreshment. By the end of the 1930's he had progressed to motorised transport, and noisily transversed the street in his conveyance, which was actually a small van built on to a motor bike frame and engine, quite popular in those days.

Tinkers have to be licenced, and are required by law to walk with their wares from town to town. I doubt if any of them ever bothered with a licence, but they did walk, they had to, there was no other way of getting around.

I often watched the grinders, perched on their high-platform push-cart, furiously peddling the motive power to the grindwheels. None of the scissors, shears, or saws, ever seem to be of any use, after being subjected to their expertise. Still a small, but steady, trickle of hopefuls, proffered up their cutting implements for, sad to say, ultimate destruction.

We suffered the usual suitcase peddlars, with shoe laces and polishes, reels of cotton and skeins of wool. For only a few pence, one could purchase a twin pack of "scenty soap", useless for washing, so mother stuck them in the chest-of-drawers, and allowed the pleasant aroma pervade through the clothes.

Edwin Eddy, from near-by Copper Hill, scratched out a precarious living, from his coal round. The two-wheeled cart was, one- donkey-power, fully loaded the poor animal was almost lifted off its legs. Still, as the load depleted with the deliveries, so the strain must have eased. Edwin was a small, but very hard man, he spoke monosyllabic, and I never saw him smile. Heaving coal is hardly an enjoyable occupation, and with only one arm, he had little to smile about.

Uninspired musicians of the mouth-organ, tin-whistle, and tone-deaf singers, walked the street, cap in hand, and picked up a few coppers. But during the summer we had a treat.

Two professional singers, a man and wife duo, sang duets from the shows, to the accompaniment of a piano-accordian. He was a light tenor, and she, a very fine contralto. They always presented themselves as if on-stage, the people of the street came to their doorways to listen. It was as near to a professional theatre, that most of them would ever get. I am indebted to Charlie Penrose, for the resuscitation of a memory that is fast failing.

The singers were called, Stewart, the husband of the duo suffered from impaired vision, and each year they appeared, it was obvious that he was slowly going blind. They had two sons, both multi-instrumentalists, but the boys were seldom seen with their parents. However, on one occasion, the family quartette gave a concert at Ventonleague Chapel, a kindly act that was much appreciated at the time.

It's a long time ago, but I can still see them, standing and singing in the street, under the hot summer sun. Immaculately attired, he in a dark suit, and sporting a bow-tie, his lady resplendent in a wide brimmed picture hat, and a long flared, floral print dress, that pirouetted around her ankles.

But I must not forget our most celebrated entertainer. The poor chap suffered a lot of "stick" from us youngsters.

"Play us a 'C' scale Joe". We gathered in a circle around the street musician, just outside Hubert Crew's house, and tormented the unfortunate.

Joe Bishop was a violinist of untapped talent, at least we had to assume he had some affinity with that difficult instrument. He carried it with him, everywhere he went, but I can't honestly say I ever heard him play a tune.

With the air of a virtuoso, he carefully tuned the four strings, then with the fiddle clamped under his chin, his countenance would glow with a dream-like smile, as the bow gently caressed the strings. A few squeaks and scratches later, Joe made his usual apology,

"Oh dear, it needs a little tuning".

By this time, of course, it was time to take around the hat.

Joe Bishop wasn't a gypsy, I suppose one could call him a tramp, a vagrant, sleeping in the hedges, or any old shelter, with Connor-Downs as his home base. On one occasion he was seen by some poachers, sleeping rough, near the golf-course at Lelant. He had walked through the poachers nets and traps, without tripping or stumbling, and was now sleeping the sleep of the innocent. They quietly crept away, and left him to his dreams.

But in his latter years, the villagers of Connor kept a closer watch on their celebrity, and installed him in a caravan, in a field off Willoughby's Lane. Local farmer, Stephen Rule, often paused at the caravan, to ensure that all was well.

One morning, Stephen looked through the window, to find the musician lying naked on the floor, his precious violin on the bunk-bed. The door was never locked, and when Stephen examined the body it was obvious that the old man had died sometime during the previous night. Why he was naked? was a mystery that was never explained.

The local builder and undertaker, Lionel Jory, called his workmen together the following morning. Joe had left no money other than a few coins, so the Council had taken over the financial responsibility of internment, with the terse instruction, "Bury him as cheaply as possible, and with the minimum of fuss". Lionel had known Joe for many years, and had no intention of burying the old man without some dignity.

"I don't want him buried in a packing case", he said, "make him a decent coffin".

So Joe was carried out in a polished wood coffin, with chrome handles and name-plate. The villagers filled the chapel, and followed the hearse, be-decked with flowers, to the cemetery. There on the hill, Joe Bishop was laid in his last resting place.

As for his beloved violin, that I never heard him play, it was placed alongside in the coffin, and buried with him.

An octogenarian voice expressed the sentiments of all who were present that day. "'e may 'av lived like a tramp, but we tilled 'im like a King".

"Bow down thine ear, O Lord, hear me; for I am poor and needy".
(Psalm 86)

9

The legend of Arnold

"Do you remember Arnold?" My friend looked at me quizzically, thought for a moment, mentally reminiscenting down the years. "Ah yes", he said, at last. "I remember him, what a character, and what a relief to us all, when he packed his bags and emigrated".

Arnold was born some sixteen years before I saw the light of day, but his name was often mentioned in conversation, so much so, that I thought I already knew him. I couldn't have been more than two years old, when I first saw the man.

He was one of a large family, no matter how hard they strived, "Lady Luck" would turn about, and they found themselves once again at the bottom of the heap.

Arnold spent his childhood days, in an atmosphere of utter despair and frustration. He always appeared to be much older than his rightful age, an old school photograph shows him in the back row, towering head and shoulders above the other children, a mischievious smile underneath a shock of dark curly hair. Today I suppose, he would be termed, a rebel, a delinquent, a drop-out. In the street he was looked upon as a character to be avoided. The few lads that befriended him, knew they had to tow-the-line, and those that summoned up the courage to oppose him, learned their lesson in no uncertain manner.

Any way-out pranks, or vandalism, there was no need to look for the offender, all fingers would point to the one-and-only. When, in 1918, St John's Street school burned to the ground, Arnold was the prime suspect, and it was the general opinion of the populous, that only his tender years saved him from the long arm of justice, and prevented his being, hung, drawn and quartered.

By the time he was sixteen, he had the appearance of a muscular, good looking lad of twenty, burning with ambition, and wanting to make his mark in the world, but there was no one to guide him, and nowhere to go. Unemployed and with little education, (he never learned to read or write) his future prospects seemed bleak, to say the least.

But he did have a glib tongue, and women were attracted to him. Mysteriously he came into possession of a leather motor-cycle helmet, goggles, and a pair of gauntlet gloves.

Walking the six miles to Camborne, he sauntered into the "Kiddley Arms", deposited his last tuppence on the bar, ordered half-a-pint of bitter, then turned his attention to the ladies, chatting them up with his usual blarney, thrilling them with stories of his prowess on the race-track. All went well, until a girl that knew him stood in front of the regulars, and told them just what he was, a compulsive liar, and a public nuisance. The infuriated speedway rider grabbed her by the throat, and would have strangled her, had not the others bundled him unceremoniously through the doorway and into the street.

But such little set-backs didn't worry him for long, and by the time that Whitsun had come around, it was a past best forgotten.

The sun was streaming down that Whit' Monday. Arnold climbed out of his bed, in the little linny room. He crouched down to avoid striking his head on the lime-washed ceiling, where it sloped down to a mere three feet from the floor, and peered out of the small window. It was a beautiful day, surprisingly so, because Whit' Mondays are so often marred by inclement weather conditions (at least it seemed so in those days).

Arnold made an instant decision, he had heard many glowing accounts about the Whitsun fair at Redruth, now at last he could go, and see for himself. After a hasty breakfast, he started out on the nine mile trek, arriving two hours later at his destination. He wasn't tired, the walk seemed to refresh him, but alas, in one respect, he was exactly as he started, absolutely skint.

This state of affairs could not be allowed to continue, a fairground is hardly the place for a penniless adventurer, not only that, he realised that his charm alone, without the necessary wherewithal would not go far in impressing the ladies. Something had to be done to redress the situation. In desperation, he looked around.

"You look like a strong lad", called the barker, from the stand outside the boxing booth.

"Who me"? answered Arnold, slightly bewildered.

"Yes you", persisted the barker. "All you have to do, is stay three rounds with my champ, and I'll give you ten shillings". Now half-a-quid in the 1920's represented a fortune indeed, to an out-of-work lad. Arnold quickly thought it over. He was useful with his fists, an early punch might do the trick, but if not, all he had to do, was stay out of trouble for three rounds, it should be easy.

"OK", he said, "I'm your man".

By this time a large crowd had collected, many of them from Hayle. Accompanied by shouts of, "We're with you boy", and, "Slay the bum", Arnold walked, like a gladiator of old, into the lions den.

They didn't bother to issue him with a full boxing kit, not even a gum shield, he was thrown a pair of ill-fitting boxing gloves, and told to strip to the waist. There was another show in twenty minutes, and time was money. The barker walked over to his champ, "It's a push over", he whispered, "Knock his bl— block off, in the first round".

The barker also turned out to be the referee, he walked to the centre of the ring.

"L-a-d-e-e-s and Gentlemen, we proudly present a three round contest, three minutes each round, in the right-hand corner our champ-e-e-n, Battling Branigan", (Boo's and cat-calls from the spectators) "In the left-hand corner your challenger, 'Ammerfist Arny". Howls of delight and cheers from the Hayle contingent. The ref' continued, "Remember folks, that if 'Ammerfist stays three rounds with our champ-e-e-n, he will receive ten shillings in prize money. He then brought the contestants to the middle of the ring.

"Now boys, I want a clean fight, no holding, touch gloves, step back, and come out fighting".

The bell gave a half-hearted clang, they touched gloves and were just about to step back, – when – it – happened –. Wham! from out of nowhere Arnold delivered a tremendous uppercut, it crashed on the boxer's jaw, almost lifting him off his feet. Dazed and bewildered he staggered blindly across the ring, ricochetted off the ropes, and fell face down on the canvas. The referee looked at his fallen protege in blank disbelief. He didn't bother to count, there was no need, boxers falling face down, do not, as a rule, recover in the stipulated count of ten.

The spectators went wild with excitement, "Arnold wins, hurrah for the new champ, give him the money ref'". At the mention of money, the ref' seemed to snap out of his stupor.

"That was a dirty bl— foul", he howled, "He's not getting any money out of me".

The mood of the spectators suddenly changed to an ominous silence.

A gent sporting a broken nose and cauliflower ears, stood up at the rear of the booth.

"Give him the ten shillings, or we'll tear your tent to pieces". Reluctantly the referee handed over the ten shillings, and again the cheers rang through the tent.

No world champion could feel more elated than Arnold, when he climbed out of the ring, and pushed his way through the jostling mob. Five minutes later, he was to be seen in the fairground, revelling in his new-found fame, with a girl on each arm. But his moment of glory was short lived, and the prize money soon dwindled away.

It was late that night, that the wanderer at last returned home, tired, once again penniless, but very, very, happy.

A month later, Arnold learned of another fair, this time at Helston. He decided that here was a golden opportunity to further his boxing career.

He walked the eight miles to Helston, and promptly booked himself as a challenger at the boxing booth. Alas his luck had run out, someone had recognised him, and passed the word on to the fight promoter.

There was to be no one-punch knock-out this time. For almost three rounds, he was battered mercilessly around the ring, and had taken so much physical punishment, that the referee had to stop the fight and count him out, while he was still on his feet. Sore, dazed, and sadly delusioned, he staggered the eight miles back to home. Opening the front door, he painfully negotiated the stairs, and collapsed on the bed.

"Are you all right boy"? his father called to him. But the only reply was a sorrowful groan. That night he resolved to retire from the noble art of self-defence, never again to climb into a boxing ring. Arnold, as they say in sporting circles, had hung up his gloves.

By the time he was seventeen years old, he proudly displayed a rather nasty scar over his right eye. How he came by that disfiguration, was a mystery to every one but himself, although my father firmly believed that the wayward lad had been on the receiving end of pick-handle, when caught in a compromising situation, by an irate husband.

It was about this time, he had a whirlwind romance with a girl from Penzance, and in a Chapel near the Morabb Gardens, they were married. Out-of-Work, with no prospects for the future, the couple settled down with the girl's parents. It was a recipe for disaster. Living in overcrowded conditions, tensions built up, and quarrels ensued. A few weeks later, he packed his bag, and walked out.

Typically he just dismissed the whole affair as if it had never happened, and seemed to forget all about it.

But six months later, he made a mistake he was to regret for the rest of his life. He fell in love again, with another girl from Penzance. It is almost unbelievable, that he actually had the effrontery to go through a marriage ceremony, with his new found love, again, in that same town, although at another Chapel. Arnold knew little about the law of bigamy, in fact it never occurred to him, that he had done anything wrong.

But his matrimonial bliss, was short lived. A few days later there was a loud knock at the door. Two stern faced men in uniform introduced themselves, and escorted the reluctant bigamist to the cold comfort of a police cell. At the magistrates court, he was referred to as, wayward, and completely lacking in any sense of moral responsibility. Arnold was sent for trial-by- jury, at the Bodmin Assises. The verdict was a foregone conclusion, "Guilty" the judge pronounced a sentence of one year in prison.

The next day Arnold was taken by train, under escort, to a first offenders prison in London.

Going to prison for a crime he never knew he had committed, would have been a traumatic experience for most people, and no doubt, our tarnished hero must have realised at last, that life's game must be played by the rules, and he, like everyone else, was subject to them. However, he seemed to accept his sojourn behind bars, philosophically, regarding it as just another experience along life's highway. With his instant wit and bland innocence, his fellow prisoners found in him a congenial companion, the "Screws" and even the warden himself, looked on with a certain amount of approval. So much so, that after eight months, Arnold was released with a remission for good behaviour. The warden had him brought to his office, and a long discussion ensued about the many pit-falls a young lad could stumble into, and advised him generally about his future conduct, and the role he should endeavour to play in society. Alas there was one obstacle that the lad could not avoid. He was three-hundred miles from home, getting a lift for such a distance would be short of a miracle, in the 1920s long-distant lorries were still a novelty, although he might manage a few short hops, here and there. The obvious mode of travel, would be the railway, but the few coins in his pocket would not take him far. There was only one course open – Shanks Pony –

The warden advised him to first head for Salisbury Plain. Some Territorials of the Duke of Cornwalls Light Infantry, were camped there, engaged on an annual military training course, he might meet up with some that he knew from Hayle, and no doubt they would help him if they possibly could.

It was a clear bright day, when the gates of the prison opened, and Arnold walked out into the sunshine, a free spirit at last.

He stopped for a meal of soup and bread at the Salvation Army, and then moved on to spend the night at a "Doss House". It was a shock to see how these down-and-outs lived, many just walked about in a methylated haze. When he awoke in the morning, the bedrooms and corridors reeked with the stench of vomit and urine. Arnold's family might have been poor, and often went without the barest necessities, but his home was clean, the brasswork on the "Slab" gleamed with pride, cleanliness is next to Godliness was the order of the day. The unfriendliness of the big city appalled him, and he was soon clear of the metropolis, heading for Salisbury Plain. Once in the country, he found the going much easier. Seeing an isolated cottage, he would knock at the door, turn on the old-world charm. Invariably the occupant would take pity on the lad, and supply him with ample refreshments. At times he would be allowed to sleep in an out-house, or a barn, but many nights were spent in the rather dubious shelter of the hedgerows. Tired and weary, he at last arrived at Salisbury Plain. It was some days since he had left the prison, and as was expected, lifts from passing motorists and carts, seldom helped more than a few miles.

The D.C.L.Is were still at the camp, and he soon located some of his old school friends. They provided him with food and shelter, and contributed to a collection to help him on his way. By the end of the week, with their training course now over, the Territorials pulled out and headed for home. Arnold found himself once again, alone, and on the road, another two-hundred miles to go.

Over the next few weeks, he slowly made his way through the countryside, at times the rain poured for many days, these were the desperate hours, holed up in some disused shack, or makeshift cover, sustaining himself as best he could, by living off the land. Then one day, he happened on a solitary cottage, just off the main road. His knock was answered by a rather good looking, middle-aged woman who invited him in. Arnold stayed in the comparative luxury of that abode for many weeks. When my father asked him what exactly he was up to in that

40

cottage, he would just cock an eyebrow, smile and say, "I chopped a lot of wood for that lady".

In the meantime the soldiers had returned to Hayle, with the latest news, "Arnold was coming home".

Sadly he was illiterate, and there had been no letter, or communication of any kind since he went "inside", but from that moment on, the folk in the street kept a weather-eye open for the returning prodigal. Being detained "at his Majesty's pleasure" seemed to have given the lad an aurora of notoriety, and his home-coming was an event not to be missed.

The story so far, is as my mother and father often recalled it, over the ensuing years, and it is from their recollections, that I have been able to tell the legend of Arnold's early days. I was only two years old when he came out of prison, and returned to the street. This was the first time, that I can honestly say, I actually recall seeing him.

It was a bright sunny afternoon, when the word "Bush telegraphed" through the street, "Arnold had been seen approaching Copperhouse" The whole of St John's Street must have been standing in their doorways, that afternoon. I peeped from behind my parents, and saw this tall man turn from Cornubia Hill, and into our street. His father, now a widower, lived in the corner house. He walked to the door and knocked, after a few moments the old man appeared, looking at his son in disbelief.

"What are you doing here boy?"

Arnold tried to explain that he had come back because there was no-where else to turn.

The old man was unrelenting, "You're nothing but a disgrace to the family and the whole street, I want nothing more to do with you, just go away and never come here again" The door slammed in the lad's face. Bewildered, he turned away, and slowly stumbled along the street,

In every close-knit community like ours, there is always one interfering, loud-mouthed, misfit, we had a prime sample in our street. The old crone stood in her doorway, and shrieked at the top of her voice, "Jail-bird, jail-bird, get out, we don't want you here".

But the other folk in the street, didn't feel that way, and had a great deal of sympathy for their wayward prodigal. It was the time of the 1926 General Strike, unemployment was rife, many of the houses were over-crowded, we ourselves, didn't live on the bread-line, we were living below it, to help Arnold represented an almost insurmountable problem.

As he came alongside our house, I saw him for the very first time.

The experience was a shock to me. Was this the Arnold I had heard so much about? – this tramp-like figure, unkempt, unshaven, wearing a very dirty, tattered, raincoat, his shoes long since worn out, stuffed with pieces of cardboard, to protect the soles of his feet. He was stumbling along like a man in a dream, tears were running down his cheeks, I never saw a grown man cry before. He shuffled, unseeingly on, and my parents stepped back inside and closed the door. Mother paused for a moment or two, then turned to father.

"I can't let him go Leonard"

Father shook his head, "Good God woman, what on earth can we do for him? four of us live here, a three-roomed house, with just the one bedroom, we've no money and very little food".

Mother looked at him in desperation, "I know he's been in a lot of trouble, but his mother and I were good friends, for the sake of her memory I can't let him go, not like this".

With a sigh of resignation, Father looked at her, "Do what you must, we'll let tomorrow look after itself".

She opened the door, by this time the lad had almost reached the Church at the junction with Cross Street. She ran out into the street and caught up with him, tapped him on the shoulder, he turned, they exchanged a few words, then walked back together to the house. Inside the front door he wearily sat in the stairs, mother hastily provided him with a cup of tea, and a little something to eat.

My parents had a long chat with him, and pointed out that he was very dirty, probably lousy, if he stayed too long he might infect the house. They advised him to spend the night in one of the hay- carts, usually to be found in an open front barn, near the Swanpool at Foundry. In the morning he could return and they would try to help him, but pointed out, they could promise nothing.

Arnold thanked them, and walked away to Foundry. That night he slept in the hay-cart.

At sun-up the next morning he was back again. Mother had risen early, the Cornish Slab roared tigerishly, with two kettles of water bubbling away on the hot-plate. He was led out into the little courtyard, to find a galvanised steel bath partially filled with cold water, soon to be topped up with the boiling water from the Slab, together with scrapings from a solidified bar of "Jeye's Fluid". – It was delousing time –

"Get off your clothes boy, and stay in that tub for at least an hour", she placed a towel and some "Puritan" soap alongside, then went back indoors and closed the curtains of the kitchen window.

Arnold sheepishly took off the tattered remnants of his clothes, and stepped into the bath. Lying there, soaking in the warm water, was a luxury he had long denied himself. Father came out of the house, walked over to the toolshed and selected a long handle fork. He stuck the fork through the pile of clothes, took them up the steps and into the garden, then burned them. Walking back to the house, he reappeared after a few minutes, with a bundle of old and very worn garments.

"I'm afraid they are rather ragged boy, but thats all we have, at least they are clean".

With no spare bed or bedding, and very little room, there was only one place for Arnold to sleep, on the floor of the small kitchen near the "Slab". For a mattress he made-do with some potato sacks, his single blanket an old army Greatcoat. But he was clean, he was warm, and above all, with friends.

He stayed with us for many months, and during that time, a noticeable change came over him. He gradually lost his devil-may- care attitude, and at last seemed to be endeavouring to re-act in a responsible manner.

Realising that we couldn't afford to feed him, he would go out and earn a few coppers, doing odd jobs, running errands, or perhaps mowing a lawn. This money, little as it was, he would give to mother, and only then would he sit with us at the scrub- top table, and share a meal. On days when he could find no work, he pretended he had already eaten at a friend's house, and refuse all offers of food. He must have been desperately hungry on many occasions. I sat with him in the kitchen, watching mother remove a cake from the oven. Unfortunately the bottom of the cake had burned, she placed the cake upside-down on a piece of brown paper, and proceeded to scrape the offending "black" from the bottom of the cake.

Arnold looked at the burnt scrapings, "Don't throw it away Mrs" he said, "I've always liked that", he lied, but not very convincingly. It was pointless to argue, and I watched as he ate the burnt ash. After that incident, mothers cakes seemed to be invariably burned, and I noticed that she no longer scraped the bottom, but instead cut it away in rather thick slices, but at the time I was too young to realise why.

Arnold was getting frustrated, he wanted to reciprocate, to do something to show his appreciation for the kindness my parents had extended to him, knowing full well, that little as it was, it necessitated a considerable sacrifice on their part. Then he had a brilliant idea, he would replenish the fuel supply by cutting some wood logs, but first of all he had to find a suitable tree. At the Foundry end of Hayle, just opposite the timber yard, there is a pleasant walk, referred to locally, as the Plantation. It consists of three pathways, in tiers, one above the other, cut into a sloping bank, and lined with Fir trees. Originally it was the site of an ancient Fort, its history now lost in antiquity.

Armed with an axe (where he got it from will be forever a mystery) Arnold proceeded to the Plantation and selected for himself a promising looking conifer. Then with youthful gusto went to work.

My Harvey the managing director of the timber yard, was sitting in his office that morning, generally at peace with the world. He could hardly believe his ears, when the sound of chopping wood came from across the road. Someone was cutting down a tree, and in broad daylight, obviously the dastardly intention of a thief or a vandal. He rushed out of his office, and across the road to the Plantation. – too late – the damage had been done, and the amateur lumberjack was seen standing triumphantly over the once- proud, but now sadly fallen, Pinus radiata.

"Good Lor' boy what have you done" Mr Harvey had recognised the axe-man instantly.

Arnold explained that he had wanted to repay, in some way, the people who had been kind to him. He couldn't work, but a goodly supply of logs for fuel, would at least be something. Mr Harvey had a long chat with the offender, and although he sympathised with the motive, he pointed out that such actions, could lead Arnold back to prison again. In any case, how on earth could he cut up a thirty foot tree, and then carry his plunder all the way back to St John's Street, a distance of just over a mile. This was a little problem, that Arnold, in his enthusiasm, had over- looked.

"Just leave it boy" said Mr Harvey, "Go home and forget all about it".

So once again Arnold returned to the street, empty handed, and once again he went hungry.

Still something had to be done, to shake off the shackles of poverty, it was simple, he would join the army. Alas, he failed the medical, his vision suffered a serious defect, in fact he was almost blind in one eye. He must have known about it for years, but it never bothered him unduly, and he never told anyone.

Utterly dismayed at this latest set-back, he returned to his usual routine, nursing a forlorn hope, that fortune was just around the corner. When one of his friends suggested emigration, the idea, with its adventurous overtones, had an instant appeal.

For some years advertisements for suitable young immigrants, had been appearing in "boys" magazines, and Arnold listened eagerly, as his friend read aloud the ad'.

"LADS"

The best life for town and country lads (16 to 20 years) is upon Australia's big prosperous farms. Greatly reduced steamship passages, only £3 payable before sailing. Government guarantees every approved boy immediately upon landing, at from 10/- to 15/- weekly, free board and lodging. Quick increases to capable workers. Every industrious lad may look forward to becoming a farmer and employer while early in life. Previous farm experience not necessary. Apply for illustrated pamphlet and full particulars to the Assistant Superintendent of Immigration for New South Wales and Victoria. 3, Melbourne Place, Strand. W.C.

This was the golden opportunity he had been looking for, a new start in another country.

Mother helped him with the correspondence, and the pamphlet duly arrived. She also insisted that any money he earned, he kept. After two months he had saved the necessary £3 and applied for the passage.

The people of Hayle had by this time, recognised in Arnold a reformed character, they opened their hearts to him, and many came forward with offers of help. A pair of shoes here, a shirt there. Mr Cannicott the local grocer on Fore Street, called to the lad, and presented him with a very smart leather suit case. Mr Ernest Pool in his drapery shop opposite, fitted him out with a new off-the-peg, brown, pinstripe, suit.

The ticket and papers duly arrived, and the day of departure finally dawned. He had only three shillings in his pocket, but looked resplendent in his polished shoes, clean starched shirt, and new suit. The old swagger and devilish glint in his eyes returned, he was himself again. With a chuckle he hoisted me on to his shoulder, and carried me across the street to Mrs Gibson's sweet shop, bought me some mints, then carried me back again. When he finally put me down, he turned to mother and said,

"Before I go, I must tell you something, it's about the school, I never intended that it should burn down, me and my mate broke in on the

45

ground floor, and made our way to the upstairs classroom. We took some exercise books from the cupboard and threw them into the open grate, then put a match to them. Some of the books must have fallen out, burning, on to the wooden floor, but we never intended it should happen that way".

Mother listened sympathetically, "Yes I know son, we all knew, but you must put that behind you now. Go out to Australia, it's a fresh start, try to make something of yourself".

Arnold picked up the leather suitcase. "With a bit of luck I'll make some real money out there, and when I come back no-one will ever dare call me Jail-bird again. I shall walk straight down the street, put my suitcase on your doorstep, and when you open the door, I'll simply say, I've come home".

He shook hands, said his goodbyes, picked up the suitcase, turned and without looking back, strode away to the station. To hide my emotion, I walked to the middle of the road, and stood there silently watching the receding figure, until it disappeared around the bend by St John's church.

A few weeks later we received a letter, it had been posted from the boat. Being illiterate presented no problem, he had fallen in with two young ladies, and one of them he "pressed" into service as his scribe. It seemed he was enjoying the voyage, and a snapshot enclosed, shows a laughing Arnold, with a beautiful girl on each arm. My father took one look at the photograph, shook his head in mock resignation. "Typical", was all he said.

More than six months passed since Arnold had left for Australia, but other than that one letter, there had been no news of him. Mother was by this time, very concerned, and she wrote to Melbourne Place hoping they might have some information of his where-a-bouts. They couldn't help, but suggested she write direct to the Commonwealth of New South Wales. From fragments of information gleaned over the next eighteen months, she pieced together the final chapter of Arnold's story.

It seemed he was soon deluded with the arduous daily grind on the farm, and decided to terminate his contract by the simple procedure of walking out. High wages were being paid on the mines, three hundred miles away, he had walked that distance once before, the journey held no terrors for him. One morning he packed his case, bade his mates "Cheerio", and walked off the farm.

He walked through the township, and on into the "Bush". Walked out into the wilderness to seek his fortune, and was never seen again.

But I'll never forget the day he walked through St John's Street, in that awful condition, spurned by his father, and the old crone screaming at him, "Jailbird, jailbird". I was only two years old at the time, but I can still see it as if it was only yesterday. And I also remember the woman, who was poor, with nothing to give except a little compassion. Alone she stepped into the street, ran after the lad, touched him on the shoulder, and when he turned his tearstained face towards her, she said the only three words he wanted to hear.

"Welcome home son".

"He went out, not knowing wither he went"
Hebrews, 11:8

10

"I'll have my supper now"

It was going to be a bleak Christmas at No 22. Father suffered all of his adult life from varicose ulcers in the legs. Now with phlebitis developing, there was only one recourse, bedridden for six weeks.

I compared his legs with the half-rotten apples, sold off very cheaply, or given away, by the greengrocers. When I told him he had "bit gone" legs, he laughed and said, "You're right boy, that's a good name for them". He was in the Territorials just before the 1914 war, but failed his medical for regular military service.

In the 1930's, with the breadwinner out of work, a family of four, like ours, could, with careful and frugal planning, just about manage on the "dole" (Approx' 30/- a week). But the sick benefit, of 15/-, offered little relief to those with no other income.

To be avoided at all cost, was the "Means Test", striking fear to all but the stoutest of hearts. When the claims to other meagre benefits had run their course, the "Means Test" could be brought into play. But first any saleable assets must be auctioned off. The so-called luxury goods (gramophones and pianos) were the prime targets of the bailiffs. Needless to say, every one in the street avoided the "Test" like a plague. My father had a few close encounters, but managed to avoid the twelfth hour, by finding some employment, just enough to top-up his depleted stamp card.

Of course there was the Church. A little money of up to 10/- a week might be allocated from the Parish Fund, but the splendiferous vicarages, that dotted the countryside, showed little understanding or compassion, indeed some who received the "Parish" found, years later, a nasty sting in its tail. Rumour of an expected small inheritance, brought the Church pounding at the door, demanding their money back – or else –

> The rich man in his castle,
> The poor man at his gate,

He made them high and lowly,
And ordered their estate.
From; "Hymns for little children"
by Francis Humphrey – 1848 –
(Married Rev Alexander 1850)

What happened to our 15/- "sick benefit" that Christmas, I never knew, for some mysterious reason, we didn't receive it. With our meagre savings now dribbled away, we had only the 6/- from the "Rechabite" sick insurance to fall back on. A contribution of three-pence a week had at least assured us of that much.

The afternoon of December 24th found my mother seated at the kitchen table, with pencil and paper, muttering aloud. "One and six for the rent, coal and paraffin 2/-, The fresh daily milk was a bit expensive, she would ask the milkman to deliver "scald" in future, at half the price. She dropped the pencil, this time it wasn't going to add up. Mother had always prided herself, that she could pull through these periods of shortages, but not this time, father had been ill too long. She turned to me, "I know you're too young to understand, but this time there is no way out. Tomorrow is Christmas, and all I have for us to eat is a few potatoes and a little bread, it will be the Workhouse for your father and me, you and your brother will have to go into a home. When the man comes with the 6/- I'll have sixpence to spare, I'll take this to the butchers, and get some meat, we'll have to see what can be done with that".

The "man" she referred to, was a carpenter and builder from Ventonleague, Sam John Coombe. Sam ran his insurance agency only as a part time business. A sincere Methodist, and a stalwart of the Copperhouse Chapel, he considered that his charity to others, was of concern only to himself and the friend-in-need. Many of his acts of kindness only came to light, years after he had passed on.

We waited all afternoon for Sam, but he didn't turn up until the evening. The door suddenly burst open, and in he walked. "Hello, hello" he said, "Why the long faces? it's Christmas tomorrow, must make the best of things" He paused, realising that he had inadvertently put his foot in it. He continued, less enthusiastically, if not rather lamely. "Er' – what are you having for Christmas dinner, roast and chicken I suppose? He looked around at the stillness of the room. Mother regarded him steadfastly, and then quietly and with deliberation. "We haven't even got a rabbit, only a few potatoes and a little bread, the coal burning in the 'slab' is the last, from now on I'll have to pick up stick, to keep it going" Mother continued, "We have been waiting for you to come with the 6/-, I was going to use a few pence of that to buy a little meat, but it's too late now, the shop is shut"

Sam stammered, "I could have come before, no-one told me, I didn't know"

"I don't suppose they have" said mother, "I've told nobody, and I never intended telling you" Bitterly she went on, "God's in his heaven, all's right with the world. It's not all right Sam, it's all dam' well wrong"

A very embarrassed Sam placed the money on the table, muttered an apology and some religious platitude, then quietly left the room.

Mother prepared the evening meal, "Sops". Broken pieces of bread, soaked in hot water, flavoured with liberal dashes of salt and pepper, with a spot of marge' or dripping added as a final touch, giving the "pretend" soup an oily effect. It was the stable diet for many families in the street at that time. It was hot and filling, but one could hardly call it nourishing. When even an Oxo cube was too expensive, "Sops" was the last and only resort.

With the evening meal over, (there were no "afters") mother set about washing the few dishes, in an enamel bowl. Suddenly the front door opened again, and Sam walked back into the kitchen. "Here you are" he said, plumping a massive rooster on the table. Then with a twinkle in his eye, "A little something to go with it" From a shopping bag he produced a large Christmas pudding. "Don't be afraid to eat that" he smiled, "I know who made it, and it's going to be a beauty"

The next day was Christmas, mother had cut a Holly bush from some unsuspecting farm hedge, and I had decorated it with bits of coloured paper and cotton reels wrapped in silver foil, salvaged from empty cigarette packets found discarded in the street. It was a far better Christmas dinner than we could have dreamed of. Some bread, potato, ample portion of chicken, followed by a liberal helping of pudding. My mother summed it up when she turned to me and said. "That's what people mean when they talk about a 'Good Samaritan'".

Some years later, my mother and Sam's wife Nellie, were talking about it. Until then, Nellie never knew who were involved, Sam never told her. Nellie takes up the story.

"It was an awful night, cold and blustery. Sam came back from his rounds, fed up, and obviously very tired. I had a hot supper keeping warm on the slab. He took off his jacket and sat at the table, but when I put the roast dinner before him, he just stared at it. I asked him if he was feeling ill, he simply replied, "I can't eat it, I've left a family who have almost nothing at all" I gave him a few minutes to compose himself, and then spoke to him. "You've got to do something Sam, it's getting late, so do it now" He got up from the table, went to the bottom of the garden and killed the largest rooster in the pen. "I'll give them this" he said. I ran into the house and fetched one of my Christmas puddings and thrust it into a shopping bag, "Give them this as well". Twenty minutes later Sam returned, he was looking much better, as if a great worry had been lifted from him, and I patiently waited to hear the story, and who were involved, but he never told me. He took off his jacket, sat at the table, smiled and said.

"They'll be alright, I'll have my supper now"

11

Found drowned

The policeman's lot was a tiresome one. His sole purpose in life was to protect the affluent, and keep the underlings (like ourselves) in their place. These are not my words, but are the views of retired law officers, when they have appeared on T.V. or interviewed by a newspaper.

Father had sold his Matchless two-stroke motor bike for £10, an aquisition that was expected to solve his conveyance problems, to and from work. But one had to be an adept engineer to keep that contraption in working order, but he was not mechanically inclined, the result being, that the old two-speed Armstrong push-bike was taken out of retirement, and pressed into service, again and again. An exercise that he described as, "riding a concrete block". With the £10 he decided to invest in one of the best roadster push-bikes available at that time.

The "Sunbeam Royal" was twice as expensive as the normal run-of-the-mill bicycle, with a lifetime guarantee. It was a heavy steed, with it's oil-bath chain case and 27 inch wheels, but surprisingly a very easy ride. The Sunbeam was always kept in prime condition, the brakes, bearings, and Sturmey Archer -K4- speed, constantly adjusted, cleaned and oiled, for optimum performance.

He was breezing down Connor Hill, at a comfortable 25 miles per hour, when his pride and joy was brought to a sudden stop by a man in blue, waving his arms like a windmill.

"Get off", said the law enforcer.

Father, a little puzzled, dutifully obeyed.

"Too many of you people riding around on bikes only fit for the scrap heap", continued the policeman, and then proceeded to check the Sunbeam, with particular attention to the brakes, by riding it up and down.

It was like waving a red flag to a bull. Father fumed as he watched his proud steed being subjected to such an indignity. He promptly walked across to the policeman's bike and checked that, in a similar

52

manner. When he finally climbed back on the Sunbeam, he turned to the red-faced arm of the law, and said,

"Don't you EVER touch my bike again".

It has often been said, that a Cornishman never forgets, and will never forgive. As far as my father was concerned, there was a hate relationship with the law and officialdom, as far back as 1917. A faded newspaper cutting, undated and unidentified, helps to put us in the picture.

Found Drowned At Hayle.
a carpenter's discovery at Carnsew Pool.

Mr Ed, Boase county coroner held an inquest at Hayle on Tuesday, on the body of an unknown male person. Mr John Opie was elected foreman of the jury. Leonard Philp, carpenter of Bodriggy St, Copperhoouse, said he was walking along the bank of Carnsew Pool on Sunday afternoon, when, the tide being out, he saw an object lying on the side of the pool near the timber yard. He went down and found it to be the body of a man, whom he did not recognise. The body was fully dressed with the exception of a hat. He reported the discovery to the police, who removed the body to the mortuary.

P.C. Wherry, who took charge of the body from the previous witness, did not recognise it. He made extensive enquiries in the neighbourhood. There was nothing in the pockets to suggest identity. On the body he found scraps of paper, old envelopes, and a child's school book (with no name), a telegram form, pieces of cake, and bread, and butter, 6d in coppers, a pair of spectacles, wooden spoon, tin teaspoon, and some short ends of cigarettes. On the telegram form the words, "Morrish, Trewellard" were to be seen indistinctly, but there was no one missing from that locality according to the policeman there. Altogether the body had the appearance of being that of an old tramp on the road. Dr Mudge, who made an examination of the body, said death was due to drowning, the body badly nourished, was that of a man about 65 years of age, and on it were no anti-mortem marks of any kind except injuries caused by crabs. He had been dead about 24 hours.

The jury returned a verdict of "Found Drowned".

Mr Geo Newton (a juror) wondered if it was an opportune time to make a suggestion to the two councils that Hayle should have an ambulance. In this case the police had to go and look all over the place for a handcart. That should not have been in a town like Hayle.

53

Dr Mudge: We ought to have a wheel ambulance.

P.C. Wherry said at present they had only a stretcher, and it was "mighty hard work" for two constables to carry it.

The Foreman of the jury (Mr Opie) undertook to ventilate the matter at the next meeting of Phillack Council, who would probably communicate with the Hayle Council.

I have given the full newspaper account, exactly as printed, edited, as it must have been, from a much larger draft. Carrying a body through the town on a handcart, was the accepted mode of transport in 1917.

What was left out of the report was the fact that my mother was also at the scene. She was carrying her first-born at the time, probably because of that she was never called as a witness. They were returning from a stroll along the weir, and decided to walk around Carnsew Pool, before going home, but hadn't gone far when they sighted the grisly find. But the newspaper story said nothing about the cross-examination that father was subjected to.

He told me, "I was only 20 years old at the time, and a bit green behind the gills. I couldn't really understand what was happening, after all, I had reported the finding to the authorities, now I found myself in a courtroom, in front of a jury, bombarded by their questions, "why – where – how", one of the inquisitors actually accused me of knowing more about the dead man, than I cared to admit, and even hinted that I could have been party to his demise. Today I would have told them to "kiss my backside", and walked out, but in 1917 I just didn't know how to handle it".

However the tide never goes out, unless it comes in again, and Francis Leonard harboured a grudge, and thirsted for revenge, for the rest of his life.

Many little incidents occurred during the 1920s and 1930s, which seemed to amuse him, such as the bicycle inspection. Then the law pounced again. He was standing alone on Cornubia corner and witnessed a speeding motor cyclist racing through the town. Unfortunately a policeman was nearby and knew the offender, but with only pedal power, he was hardly in a position to give chase.

Once again F.L. was dragged reluctantly into court, thoroughly brainwashed into saying the right answers to the expected questions. After all, it was a big case, probably the only one Hayle had that year, nothing must be allowed to go wrong (visions of promotion no doubt)

Father's appearance in the dock was an absolute farce. He reversed his statements and made nonsense of all the carefully planned prosecution, so much so, that the exasperated magistrate threw the case out.

Outside the court the sergeant grabbed the grinning witness by the coat lapels. "You did it deliberately", he roared, "Made us look like bl— fools.

Father removed the policeman's grasping hands, and quietly replied.

"That's just a little in return, for what you did to me in 1917". But the police still had a card up their sleeve, they kept him waiting many months for his few shillings expenses.

12

Ad astra

Young lads have always been fascinated by mechanical inventions, especially if there is also a mystery involved, and I was no exception. Since the 1920s, vague references to the Connor Downs helicopter were hinted at, but no-one seemed able to give substance to the enigma. My mother "pooh-hooed" the suggestion that a vertical-take-off flying machine, was made, and flew, on the hill.

"Load of nonsense", she snapped.

Father didn't reject the stories off-hand, but cautiously answered with a tactful, "Perhaps, or might-have-been".

But 50 years later there was a witness, a retired farmer. I often saw him tending a vegetable patch alongside Burnt House Lane, and gave him a lift on numerous occasions, on way to my work.

Stephen Rule, (the same who closed the Joe Bishop story) filled in the details of the flying machine.

"Just after the First-World-War, Jack Rickard returned from America, where over a period of a few years he had accumulated a fair sum of money, and purchased Little Connorton Farm at Connor-Downs. There was a fervour throughout the country at that time, to discover the secrets of vertical-take-off flight. Newspapers offered large sums of money, to the successful innovator, the race was on, and Jack was caught up on the tide of enthusiasm. He set-to on the drawing board, burning the midnight oil for many weeks, until finally, a working design took shape. The machine wasn't large enough to carry a pilot, but was in fact a large model.

It was now necessary to get a helping hand to assist with the building and assembly. He recalled employing Jan Barber, a willing handyman, from Nankervis, Ventonleague. When approached, Jan volunteered his services, and they both spent many long hours in the barn at Connor-Downs. Slowly the weird and wonderful machine of the future, took shape.

The power plant was an old motor-bike engine, and this was fastened to a wooden platform. Four tubular supports bolted to the platform, curved inwards over the engine and supported a bearing to the vertical drive shaft. The shaft being coupled to the engine via a chain drive and bevel gearing, then finally to the rotors.

There was of course, much more to the design, than these few sparse and vague details, but as far as I know, no drawings or photographs remain today.

The day for testing finally arrived, and on a beautiful summer's evening, the helicopter was driven by horse and cart, to the slopes of Roseworthy valley, with its solitary, ivy-covered, old mine stack, standing like a sentinel, watching over all.

It had been agreed that the helicopter would slowly be let out on a 100 foot rope from a ratchet hand winch, securely staked to the ground.

Loud and long the spectators cheered, when the engine spluttered into life. Slowly the machine lifted itself from terra-firma, and ascended gracefully, but noisily, into the heavens. At the end of the tether, it hovered, slightly swaying, there was no spinning, all seemed to be under perfect control. Had the fuel run out, disaster would have ensued, so after 10 minutes the machine was winched back to safety. Jack and Jan congratulated themselves on its unqualified success.

Now to take the business a stage further.

A patents broker had just opened an office in Camborne, and he offered to act as agent, and patent the designs as quickly as possible. Jack left the drawings in his capable hands, and waited – and waited – and waited.

Later, after numerous enquiries, he received a letter from a solicitor, informing him that the patents had been registered in the broker's name, and then sold to a "foreign" concern. Moreover, Jack had no legal right or claim on the designs, and must not under any circumstances continue experiments on similar lines, infringement of patent law could lead to a costly legal action.

Infuriated, Jack grabbed a knife, harnessed the pony and trap, and drove hell-for-leather to Camborne. But the impending death wish was never carried out, the bird had "flown-the-coop".

Thoroughly dejected, the inventor returned to the farm, smashed the helicopter with a sledge hammer, throwing the shattered pieces into the corner of the barn. And there, some 30 years later, Stephen Rule re-discovered the broken odd-ments, while clearing out the barn. Little remained that was recognisable, some pieces of bent tubing, parts of a motor-bike engine, and one of the rotors. The latter was made from sheet aluminium, and beaten into a flattened oval section, with a rivetted joint.

But did Jack Rickard actually invent the first successful helicopter? His experiments seem to have been carried out, about 1920. It appears that his machine did in fact, rise vertically and remain for some time almost motionless in the air, without spinning around. Also that he had hit on the idea of a revolving wing, rather than a prop' (the rigid rotors of the earlier inventors, had been a recipe for disaster) Did he hinge the rotors near the centre, to allow the blades to flap up and down, according to the direction of the motion? We shall never know.

In 1923 Juan de la Cierva developed an autogyro with a rotary wing, this was the forerunner of these machines.

In 1929 an autogyro of advanced design took to the skies. With a top speed of 94 mph, from its Genet major engine, and able to land in only 5 yards, it was at last accepted as a viable form of air transport.

But autogyros need a short run to take-off and land, the helicopter, as we know it today, was still in the distant future.

Nothing, we are told, is new.

From the yellowing pages of the now defunct "Boys Own Paper" we read;

"In 1875 a steam driven helicopter made a 20 second flight of some 15 metres". Hardly a world shattering achievement, but still it was a start.

The "Bard" neatly summed it up, when he wrote;

"There is more in Heaven and earth than meets your philosophy – '

13

Late lamented

"I've helped to bury hundreds of them", my father spoke quietly from his chair. "But", he continued, "I've always hated the thought of it, and I don't suppose I'll ever feel any differently about it".

He had just returned from a funeral, and as always on these occasions, he became a little withdrawn, and I suppose, saddened by the futility of it all.

Most building contractors, acted as undertakers, when the situation demanded. It proved to be quite a remunerative sideline, to their usual building and repair business.

Regardless of his repugnance, father seemed quite good at making coffins, with an output of two in one day if required. It was very hard work, when one considers that the timbers were cut from one inch thick rough planks of elm, oak, or similar medium or hard wood. They were then hand planed, cut to size, scarfed, bent, and finally assembled. Ned Coombe, father's boss and mentor, during his apprenticeship, always insisted on using prime knott-free timber, But others were not so fussy, and the knotts would be knocked out, the holes made good by plugging. The faulty piece of timber would be utilised for the bottom, on the assumption that no-one ever turned a coffin over to inspect the bottom. The inside of the box was then painted with hot pitch, a precaution deemed necessary, to prevent body fluids from getting out. Nothing more unpleasant or embarrassing to an undertaker, than a "dropsy" victim leaking all the way to the church, and on to the graveside. A happening that was not unknown.

As a further precaution, Ned packed the bodies in flour, although I have never heard of any one else doing this, but he could boast, and guarantee, a dry box.

Finally, the inside of the coffin was padded and lined with white linen. (such luxuries as silk were unheard of in Hayle)

The carpenters. employed in this business, naturally swapped yarns with each other, and some of the stories that I heard, were bizarre to say the least. Someone made a mistake with the measurement, the box was too short for the body, but the corpse fitted perfectly, after the legs had been broken.

Another cadaver was so bloated with "dropsy" that drastic measures were necessary. A screwdriver was stuck into the swollen leg and the water drained off into a bucket, and it happened on more than one occasion.

The old tramp who committed suicide, by putting his head under the wheels of an express train, severing his neck cleanly as if cut by a butchers knife, presented little problem. A sawn-off piece of broom handle, pushed into the gullet, re-assembled the head with the body very neatly, and with a bandage around his neck, it was said that he looked better than when he was alive.

I suppose the ultimate disaster happened, (not in Hayle but a few miles away). The bearers were carrying the coffin up the pathway to the church, when suddenly it happened, the bottom dropped off.

When I recalled the unfortunate mishap, with one of the family some years later, he said;

"The old man never mentions it, and we wouldn't dare, I'm afraid it's a shame that he will take to his grave".

It is not generally known, that if a doctor has been in regular attendance to one who is terminally ill, he may not be required by law, to examine the deceased before issuing a death certificate. And so it was with "Bit O String". The old man had obviously only a few hours, before crossing the great divide. When this happened the son was instructed to come along to the surgery, and collect the certificate. All went as planned, and the next day the undertakers carefully rested the "dear departed" in the coffin.

Then the unexpected happened, B.O.S suddenly sat bolt upright, shouting at the top of his voice.

"What the bl— h— is going on here?"

Many young apprentices suffered purgatory, during their first year, and stories of the torment they were subjected to, seem almost unbelievable today.

The mid-day dinner hour, was a convenient period for the 'initiation. The unsuspecting victim was suddenly grabbed and bundled into a coffin, the grinning pranksters sitting on the lid, while gleefully munching their pasties.

In retrospect it was a cruel and stupid prank, but as a young lad I laughed along with the others, when I heard such stories.

It didn't seem quite so funny, when in 1939 at the tender age of 14, I found myself in the box.

Many old cottages had very narrow, rickety, and winding staircases, making it impossible to manoeuvre the coffin, either to, or from, the bedroom. Some cottages had solved the problem by incorporating a coffin size trap-door in the bedroom floor.

The old three storey house near the "Bridge" had no such convenience. A series of ladders were tied together until they reached the uppermost floor. The sash was removed from the box- frame window, and the coffin carefully lowered by ropes down the ladders. Mission safely accomplished, all involved heaved a sigh of relief.

Father hated collecting corpses for burying, from the work- houses. They were so emaciated, he described them as looking like parchment stretched over wire-netting. "My God", I often heard him say, "didn't they ever feed them?"

But a worse shock was to follow. Father arrived too early at the Mortuary to collect a cadaver, only to find the caretaker happily sewing up the corpse with mail-bag stitches, the best his unskilled hands could manage, alongside was a bloodied bucket with some torn human remnants. Cheerfully he explained, that the pathologist never carried out the surgery, but simply told him (the caretaker) the organs required, and left him to his grisly work. When father pointed out the shock and anguish that relatives might experience, if they ever examined the body, and saw this carnage, the caretaker laughed and said.

"Would you strip a body, just to look at it?"

Point taken – But looking back over these pages, I can understand a little of how my father must have felt.

Mother would say. "Leave him alone".

And that's what we did.

61

14

Taxi!

"Frings" was a part-time taxi driver, working on behalf of his father. Short in stature, lean of countenance, he shortsightedly stared at everything and everybody, through thick lens spectacles, framed in tortoiseshell.

I can't remember what his main source of income was, but I was told that at one time he was landlord of a small pub.

If he was ever involved in an accident with another car, I never heard about it, which may seem surprising, having regard to his defective eyesight. However there are two reasons for this.

(1) He seldom exceeded 20 miles per hour.

(2) Other drivers had a tendency to change to another route, whenever he hove into view.

Of course he wasn't christened "Frings", but the Cornish with their delight of nick-names, gave him that label, and it stuck.

Actually the name came about because of a very serious incident, it could hardly be called an accident, perhaps a mishap would be a better expression.

He had received orders from his father, to take the taxi to Hayle station, and there, pick up a Mr Quinn who was returning from America.

The old taxi coughed and spluttered up the hill to the station, parking itself outside the main entrance. He applied the hand-brake and stepped down from the running-board. Affectionately he gazed at the ancient monstrosity, gave the brass radiator cap a deft rub with his handkerchief, then casually strolled through the waiting-room and on to the platform. The train was sweeping around the curve under the bridge, and about to stop on the "down" line.

He remembered Mr Quinn from a few years previously, so he had no difficulty in recognising the distinguished gentleman that alighted from the carriage. With his introductory remarks well rehearsed (at least mentally) the taximan stepped forward, addressing the object of his intentions with the aplomb of a Shakespearian actor.

"Welcome Sir, welcome indeed back to Hayle". He didn't get any further, the dramatic effect of his opening remarks was somewhat spoiled by a young urchin running, panting, up the platform. "Hey mister – mister".

The taximan paused, wrathfully glaring through his thick lenses.

"What is it boy?" he thundered, "speak your piece and be off"

"Er – ' stammered the lad, "was that your car outside mister".

"If you are referring to the large black saloon, the answer my boy, is in the affirmative".

"Well", replied the lad, with a surpressed giggle, "e's just gon' down the 'ill".

It took about 3 seconds for this intelligence to sink in and take effect. Mr Quinn suddenly found himself alone on the platform, his two suitcases having been dropped and dumped, to the detriment of any breakables inside. The urchin and the taximan reached the station yard in record time, alas it was empty – panic ensued – with terror in his heart he turned and raced toward the hill, and half-way down where it curved, the awful moment of truth was confirmed. Sticking out of a boundry wall was the rear half of what might have been, a large black elegant saloon. The dust was already settling on the tangled wreckage of steel, glass, and rubble, one look at the catastrophe was enough for him to realise, that he would never again sit at the wheel of that conveyance. A small assembly of inquisitive on-lookers soon gathered, and after about 20 minutes, his father appeared, someone had obviously, and gleefully, reported all. Such news travelled fast in Hayle.

His Pater viewed the wreckage in disbelief. The saloon had crashed through the wall like an army tank, entirely demolishing an outdoor lavatory, before finally wheezing its "last", like a mortally wounded dinosaur.

"My boy, my boy,, what have you done?" remonstrated the old man, the object of his wrath stood with tear-filled eyes.

"I don't know what happened 'Favor', (t and h in combination had always been troublesome) "the vibration of the train must have released the hand-brake". Vainly he searched for some word of consolation, but none were forthcoming. The old man stood apoplectic with grief, weakly the taximan continued, "Now then 'Favor' don't upset yourself, remember your heart condition", then with a flash of inspiration he added, "after all, 'frings' will happen, and 'frings' will happen, there's 'nuffink' we can do about it". From that moment the local wags re-christened him, "Frings will happen" or "Frings" for short, a name that he was to carry to his last resting place.

For many years after his father had passed on, "Frings" carried on the taxi business, his latest aquisition a large outlandish contraption, whose ancestry was lost in history.

Being short-sighted was a decided drawback for a taxi driver, especially in inclement weather conditions. Bringing the "Hayle Merry-makers" back from a concert, proved a nightmare for all concerned. The blanket of fog lay quite thick in places along the country lanes, the old taxi chugging bravely along at less than walking pace. Numerous were the stops, and "Frings" would climb out from behind the wheel, walk around the vehicle, and peer unseeingly into the gloom.

"What's up boy?" asked a voice from the back seat.

"Nuffink to worry about", returned the driver, trying to exude an aura of self-confidence that had long since deserted him. "Just looking around to make sure we are still on the road, after all" he added, "we don't want to end up in a field do we?" His attempt at a weak joke was not received as well as he thought it might, in fact it was greeted by a dead silence. "Frings" climbed back into the taxi, "Sorry about that folks, you know if it hadn't been for this fog, I'd 'skeech' home".

The voice at back stirred again, it was Norrie Quinn, the comedian. "Just 'skeech' along quietly boy, you're doing a wonderful job".

Norrie again closed his eyes, and returned to his silent prayer. Much later the concert party reached their destination, mentally shattered and on the verge of a serious breakdown. Still the taxi-driver had delivered them, more or less, in one piece, and for that at least they were thankful.

I had heard him often say, "The greatest pleasure in this world, is sitting behind the wheel of a Daimler, and smoking a Woodbine". Alas his smoking habit seldom met with the approval of his passengers. He had the most disconcerting habit of sticking his cigarette hand out of the nearside window, and sit gazing, mesmerized, at the burning weed. This might seem fairly harmless in itself, except that he would be driving at the time.

During the summer months, there was some holiday trade, in and about the town, and he was often busy taking the newly arrived visitors, from the station to the "Huts" (we never called them "Chalets") on the Towans, less than a mile away. It was a journey they were never to forget. "Frings" would be so engrossed in the burning cigarette, that his passengers finally descended from the vehicle, shaking from head to foot, their joyous holiday spirit reduced to ruins, before they had even started.

Typical, was the oft' told story of the Hayle Cricket Team. The team had been playing fairly well, and fully expected to give Newlyn a thrashing that was long overdue. But their expectations of victory did not take into account the taximan with his ever- present Woodbine. The usual mental and moral disintegration followed, and when the taxi almost plunged off the quay at Penzance, with one wheel hanging in the void, the proverbial camels back was finally broken. Dispirited, the team returned from Newlyn, after losing the match. A shameful defeat, long remembered.

The last time I saw "Frings" and his taxi, he was driving along Commercial Road, strangely devoid of other traffic. That rapturous smile, transfixed on the glowing Woodbine, still peering behind the pebble glasses. I watched as he "skeeched" along in a cloud of smoke at a steady 20 miles per hour, and thought to myself,

"There goes a man at peace with the world."

15

Against all odds

Cardell Hewart had no legs, – well – he had two fleshy stumps which helped him to keep balance, when he sat on a chair, just for a laugh he would lift them up to his neck.

Where others walked – he crawled.

Cardell was born this way and in his early days lived with the Harvey's at Trevassack, near Highlanes.

Even as a young lad, he refused to give in to his deformity. My father remembers him making a "Butt" for himself, out of an apple box, a plank, and four discarded pram wheels. He was now mobile, and able to get around, even to the town and to school.

I knew him when he was much older, and living (on his own) on the edge of Highlanes. The story goes that the locals had clubbed together to buy him a single-roomed hut, complete with a small American stove. The Phillack Parish Council allowed him a site alongside the road. At last he was truly independent, except that the "Butt" had long gone and he was back to crawling about again. The good people of Highlanes decided to remedy the situation, and presented him with a wheelchair. Independent though he tried to be, Cardell was not without friends.

The invalid chair of the 1920's and 1930's was a much different affair from the light aluminium design of today.

It had a wooden bucket seat, with two large diameter wheels, sporting narrow solid tyres, at the rear. (By the late 1930's these wheels had been superceded by bicycle wheels with pneumatic tyres). The smaller wheel at the front, was hand-cranked by a long tiller bar which also acted as the steering handle. The contraption worked fairly well when travelling on the flat, but Cardell found he could get better traction by turning the rear wheels with his hands, when attempting an up-hill climb. With all this effort, his arms became very strong and muscular, but "Killing House Lane" from Bodriggy School to High Lanes, was a bit much even for Cardell's arms. The hill had never had any attention that I knew of, and the journey to the top, with its large stones, bumps and pits, was decidedly hazardous to all who ventured forth. Cardell refused to be thwarted by this obstacle, and often, cunningly, timed his home-ward journey to coincide with us boys leaving school.

Suddenly, and without warning, we found ourselves press-ganged into providing the necessary motive power. Gosh! was he heavy? we suffered his cajoling and abuse, as we bent to our unwanted task. "Come on – push you s—", and other niceties, until, with a sigh of relief, his "lordship" finally arrived at his destination. Not only did we have to push Hayle's most celebrated citizen, but his dog also, sitting comfortably just behind him.

No one could say he was lazy. He topped-up his meagre pension by doing odd jobs. Harry ("aily") Watling (a local preacher) had a workship on Cornubia Hill, tapping boots, and Cardell would make a few coppers fetching and carrying boots and shoes for him. The cinema gave him a job tearing tickets, and showing the patrons to their seats. We looked upon the scene as norm', but holiday visitors were shocked and disgusted to find an employee crawling about on the floor, and pulling himself around by the chair arms. They objected bitterly, but their objections were totally ignored.

He was the proud possessor of a 12 bore single barrel shot gun, which he could use to good effect. Peering through the bars of a five bar gate, he would spot a rabbit, shoot from that position, then drop the gun and crawl out to his prey, returning with the lifeless animal in his mouth.

Cardell had a wicked sense of humour, which at times went a little too far. At one time he was seen in the street, sporting a black eye. Well, he had always wanted to be one of the boys, and if you dish it out, you have to be prepared to take it.

Cardell's conveyance squeaked to a stop on the Causeway, he fancied a wild duck for supper, and had come armed with his trusty shotgun, the only snag, was how to get to the middle of the mud flats, and still be reasonably clean. The problem solved itself when he spotted two acquaintances, and quickly conscripted them to act as porters, and carry him to a convenient hide-a-way, a sandy hollow in the centre of the tidal flats. All seemed well, Cardell was now in position and fairly clean into the bargain. The two disgruntled porters returned, mud splattered, to the Causeway to watch "Mein Sahib" in action.

Too late the hunter realised he had badly mistimed his shooting expedition, the tide was coming in.

"Get me out of this", roared the marksman, but the two on the Causeway just grinned and continued to watch the drama unfold. Cardell was a fair swimmer, considering his disability, and it wasn't long before he found himself floundering in the water. With no help forthcoming there was only one alternative – Swim – With a dog-paddle stroke, he made for the shore, and that wasn't easy, trying as he was, to keep his gun clear of the drink. At last he crawled out of the water, "Now I'm going to deal with you s—" he howled, but before he could take aim and pull the trigger, his tormentors had prudently vanished.

Killing House Lane, was finally surfaced after World War 2, the council gave Cardell the job of night watchman, the workmen leaving their tools and road making equipment by the side of his hut. I sat with him by the brazier one evening. "You know Des", he said, "for the first time in my life, I've got a real job". I knew what he meant, he was now an equal. The Cardell Hewart that I knew, was a man of great courage, dependent on no one but himself. A man who had little or nothing, and asked for no more.

A member of the "Old Cornwall Society" spoke bitterly to me. "It's a d— shame, the things that are being written about Cardell, now he is no longer here to defend himself".

"Perhaps", I replied. "I'll write something to redress the anomaly".

"Our soul is exceedingly filled with the scorning
of those that are at ease, and with the contempt
of the proud".

Psalm, 123:4.

16

Garden Serenade

The Chinns (mother and daughter) hailed from Angarrack, and finally settled in a two roomed cottage at Ventonleague, alongside the stream. It had the usual outside toilet, water was available from the village well in the courtyard of a house on Caroline Row. It is doubtful if they ever used it, the climb back up the hill was rather daunting, the little stream that rippled by, just a few yards away was much more convenient. It's a long time ago, but I can just recollect the mother, she had taken to her bed, with a terminal illness. My aunt Bessie who lived alongside, often prepared a meal for her. The old lady reached out, took my aunt's hand in hers. "I'm afraid that my daughter Laura, is not a fit person to care for me". Unfortunately this was very true. Laura now in her late forties, was illiterate and backward, with the mentality of a child. When her mother finally passed away, Laura stood dazed and motionless by the graveside, she didn't cry, and after it was all over, she dismissed the whole affair as something too remote and unpleasant to be remembered, and seldom mentioned her mother again.

Laura continued to live in the little cottage, with its corrugated galvanised roof. I never saw her use the American cooking stove, fire on such a scale seemed to frighten her. For heating, frying, or boiling, she relied on a "Beatrice" paraffin stove, a number of these portable appliances, stood like sentinels around the kitchen. Laura could fill, light, and use them, but she had never learned how to trim the wicks, clean, or maintain them. Whenever they flickered or smoked, they quickly found themselves condemned to early retirement. It only needed a few broad hints around the village, and some kind benefactor would present her with yet another oil stove.

It is strange how backward people often seem to have an affinity with animals, and Laura was no exception.

In the nearby "Phoenix" warehouse, cats were encouraged to roam and breed. Cats have very clean habits, and it proved to be an effective

Ventonleague Row. 1908

and inexpensive method of controlling the vermin population. After a few generations of breeding, the felines reverted to a semi-wild state. They were seldom seen in daylight, but came out of hiding in the early morning, and late evening, emerging from their bramble jungle at the rear of the store, to go foraging for a change of diet.

Laura would rise and go to bed, with only the light in the heavens to give her a vague semblance of time, the clock in the kitchen stopped just after her mother died. She never learned to tell the time, so it was left to run down, and remained lifeless on the corner cupboard. The cats soon discovered Laura's early rising habits, and for some obscure reason, regarded her as a friend and an ally.

Just before the sun rose in the morning, they climbed the "Phoenix" boundary wall, slunk across the gardens, and squatted in a neat semi-circle, facing their foundress. Laura never attempted to touch them, but would give them a little milk from time to time, when available. Fascinated, she would watch them while sitting on a "slag" stone. Gently rocking to and fro, she quietly talked and sang to them. Her singing can only be described as a mumbled drone, the cats sat transfixed in mesmerised silence, they seemed to find a kindred spirit in Laura. Suddenly, just as the sun broke over the horizon, they stretched themselves, then one after the other, stealthily, like fugitives from justice, slunk back across the gardens, to their jungle retreat at "Phoenix".

When the neighbours asked Laura if she was ever frightened when facing these unpredictable, and potentially fierce animals, she would reply, "They waint 'arm me, and they naw I'd never 'urt 'em, you see I tock and sing to um, the're my friends".

And that was an assumption that none of us argued with.

But one morning the cats were disappointed, Laura did not put in an appearance. The neighbours were not, at first, unduly perturbed, their celebrity did on occasion, oversleep. But by the afternoon, with still no sign or sound from the cottage, it was obvious that something serious and unaccountable had happened. At six-o-clock that evening, two village stalwarts just arrived home from work, found themselves elected to make an investigation.

They cautiously approached the cottage, the door was on the latch (that was no surprise, Laura never locked her door) The kitchen was empty, and their calls brought forth no answer from the bedroom. With mounting apprehension, they opened the bedroom door, and peered into the gloom. There was Laura sitting bolt up- right in bed, her eyes wide open, staring straight ahead, as if trying to comprehend some phenomena, which escaped her limited mental capability. Recognising the voices of the stalwarts, she quickly pulled herself together and assured them that she was quite alright.

After a cursory investigation, the two elected chuckled together, the great mystery was a mystery no longer.

Some young japers in the village had tarred the only bedroom window, and Laura had sat in bed all day, waiting for the sun to come up.

But Laura never bore a grudge, some volunteers finally cleaned the window, and often she told the story to anyone who could spare a few minutes to listen. "Longest bloomin' night I ever 'ad", she said, followed by that raucous laugh of hers, which reverberated through the village.

Laura continued to live her life in her own way, seemingly oblivious to anything or anybody around her. She seldom washed, and the smell of paraffin pervaded everywhere. Cooking was limited to a simple "fry", and her meals often consisted of a cup of tea and some cakes, passed on by a kindly neighbour. Through it all she seemed remarkably healthy, as my father would say, "No germs could ever live on her".

In every close-knit community, there is always, "one not to be trusted", and Ventonleague had its fly in the ointment.

Laura never possessed any sleeping attire, and usually donned an old pull-over, before climbing into bed. The lady who approached her, pointed out that it was usual to wear a nightdress when retiring. She had booked a seat for the coming Saturday, on a "Crimson Tours" bargain hunting trip to Plymouth, and if Laura wished, she could purchase some nightdresses quite cheaply there. Laura thought it was a good idea, and foolishly handed over her week's pension of ten shillings. Suffice to say, neither the clothing or the money was ever seen again. It was some time before the shame of the confidence trick leaked out, how Laura had managed that following week, was anybody's guess.

I must digress at this point, in order to place an historical fact, into perspective.

Workhouses were first set up under the 1834 Poor Law Act. They were deliberately to look like prison fortresses, in order to deter all but the most desperate. Discipline was strict, food rations very meagre. It was a place where the old and unwanted died. Officially Workhouses ceased to exist on March 31st 1930, but the buildings continued in use, with little alteration or modernisation, under various guises. Many were designated as Old People's Homes, with orphans and foundlings occupying a far wing. At Madron, people stood in their doorways, to watch the little girls dressed in faded blue-cotton dresses, being shepherded along the back-lane to the nearest Church. As far as the watchers were concerned, the grim buildings were still Workhouses, and only after the 1948 Health Service Act, when such as at "Barncoose" were converted and extended, to reincarnate themselves into modern hospitals, did the frightening horror of the Victorian Workhouse, recede into history.

But now back to Laura, who was soon to suffer a traumatic experience.

The "League of Dirty Tricks" held a clandestine get-to-gether, the sole object of the meeting, was to remove, once and for all, an unsightly blot on the landscape. The blot being namely one Laura Chinn. "After all", they reasoned, "she would be much better off in care". "Care" being one of the two Workhouses, each within a nine mile striking distance, or better still, the Asylum, fifty miles away at Bodmin. Anywhere, as long as this objectional creature was institutionalised, the quicker forgotten the better.

But it wasn't simply oiling the wheels of the Tumbrels, and carting the unfortunate away to oblivion. The ponderous workings of English law had, first of all, to be negotiated. The case against Laura had to be watertight. A member of the medical profession rallied to the cause, he would, under some pretext, call on the lady, and surreptitiously inspect her living conditions. His evidence at the tribunal, would ensure beyond doubt, the success of the venture.

Laura was indeed honoured and impressed when the nice gentleman called on her. "I've been sent along to see that you are getting along all right", he said. He didn't stay long, the dank smell of smoke and parafin, along with other undefined aromas, soon drove him out into the open. Mission accomplished, he reported to the L.O.D.T. The case against Laura was unassailable, she was already booked for the "Land of the Lost".

Some weeks later, the "bomb" dropped.

An official looking document was handed to her, Unable to read or write, she took it to a neighbour who translated the contents for her.

"Laura Chinn was to appear before a tribunal at Camborne, who would decide her future well-being".

She didn't have to be told, Laura had heard about these "in-care" places, they were the old Workhouses and Asylums. It is hard to visualise the shock that such a missive would be, to someone who was illiterate and simple. She had never been on a bus or train, in her life, and didn't even know where Camborne was, albeit, only six miles away.

In desperation she begged my mother to help her. Mother realised that Laura had been "set-up", and against all the evidence that would be presented, there was little that anyone could do. However she consented to accompany Laura to Camborne, and sit with her throughout the ordeal.

The Day arrived, the L.O.D.T sat with satisfied smirks on their faces, as their medical representative gave his evidence with glowing eloquence. "The woman Laura Chinn was totally unfit to live on her own, her mode of living can only be described as Dickensian". On and on he went, leaving Laura in shocked confusion. He couldn't resist closing his diatribe, with an invective reference to her illiteracy, and her mindless mumblings. "It has been said that she sings to cats". The jury allowed themselves a little titter at that remark, only to be quickly admolished by the chairman.

The L.O.D.T now had their "dig". "It was their opinion that this woman must be placed in "care", the quicker the better for her and everyone around her".

It was now Laura's turn to stand before the bench, and try to defend herself.

The chairman (he was probably a magistrate) was a kindly man, he looked at the distraught woman. "Now listen to me Laura, do you understand what is happening here today?"

Laura stood before him, with tears running down her face, saying over and over again, "I ebm dun nob'y no 'arm".

He turned to my mother, "You see Mrs Philp, we have a serious problem, this woman is not fit to plead, and she has no legal representation, would you speak on her behalf?" Mother protested, she had no experience in legal or court matters, but the chairman was insistent, "Just answer some questions that I shall put to you, as best you can".

"First of all Mrs Philp, tell us how you became involved?"

"I live at St John's Street, but collect the rents of two properties at Ventonleague, on behalf of my sister in America. Laura appealed to me when she received notice of the tribunal".

"Is it true that Laura lives in rather shabby and smelly conditions?"

"Yes sir, that is true".

"She doesn't appear to be undernourished, how do you account for that?"

"She has always been remarkably sturdy and fit, her food is usually plain and sparse, but seems to be sufficient for her needs. Occasionally a neighbour will cook or bake something for her as a treat".

"Does she interfere or try to intimidate her neighbours in any way?"

"No, she never imposes on anybody, keeps her own counsel most of the time, although she does mumble and swear to herself quite a lot, however, she will stand and chat with anyone who has the time to spare".

"What is this story about the cats?"

"They are half-wild, come from a nearby store, no one else can get near them, but they seem to trust her. She mumbles to them, in her sing-song way, gives them a little food, and calls them her friends.

Although there is little to give, she has this kind disposition toward animals, and they seem to respond to her".

"Mrs Philp, please tell the tribunal, how much rent Laura pays you per week?"

(I forget the exact figure, probably only a shilling, but I remember mother telling me, that all at the tribunal that day, roared with laughter, when she told them)

The chairman quickly brought the assembly to order.

"As agent for the property, acting on behalf of your sister in the USA, and having heard all the evidence to the contrary, given here today, would you be prepared, to allow Laura, to live on at Ventonleague, at this ridiculously low rent?"

At last mother could see a chink of light, at the end of the tunnel, all was not yet lost.

"Yes Sir", she replied, "but of course, if in years to come, she became terminally ill, then other arrangements would have to be made".

Laura was still crying when they brought her to the bench, for the last time. The chairman looked at her sympathetically.

"No-one is going to hurt you Laura, no-one is going to lock you away".

But Laura couldn't hear, she just stood there and sobbed,

"I ebm dun noby no 'arm".

The chairman closed the file, looked at mother and said, "Take her home Mrs Philp".

Laura soon forgot all about the sordid business, and lived on for many years, in more or less contented bliss. The introduction of an outdoor water mains, helped to ease the domestic situation.

World War 2, came and went, but Laura never really understood what it was all about. The ration books constituted a mystery, she was never to solve, fortunately the shopkeepers sorted it out for her.

After the War, it was noticeable that Laura was failing, she became more taciturn, and seen less frequently around the village. The inevitable happened, Laura was taken seriously ill. She was found in a bed saturated with urine, the dye from the jumper, she always wore at night, had stained blue, through the bedding, through the straw mattress, and on to the floor.

Laura didn't have to be told, she knew, "the writing was on the wall". It was the beginning of the end.

She didn't hesitate to sign the document, the doctor placed before her, and with a shaky hand, scratched her "cross" of acceptance on the bottom line.

An hour later the ambulance arrived to take her to "Barncoose".

My parents visited her at "Barncoose", father gave an involuntary shudder, as he passed through the old gateway. The Workhouse scenes from the past, were still vivid in his memory. But the newly formed National Health Service, had performed miracles. They found Laura in a modern ward, of just a few beds. The raucous laugh echoed through the building, when she saw them coming. Spotlessly clean, she sat up in bed, obviously enjoying the attention being lavished on her. But she quickly tired, and was soon half-asleep. Mother turned to father, "I doubt if we shall ever see her again".

The matron came to the bedside and offered to show them the new hospital, the first stage nearing completion.

And so my parents saw a "Barncoose" that was beyond their expectations, the old buildings were still "in situ", but the insides had been ripped apart. All was now light and airy, clean and up-to-date, the transformation was unbelievable. The matron stopped at a battered wooden door. "This", she said, "is the recreation room, the last of the old Workhouse".

She opened the door, and memories of more than twenty years before, came flooding back to father. The feeble and old, sat like Zombies, with their backs against the lime washed walls, staring mindlessly at the ancient "Tortoise" stove, with its chimney pipe disappearing somewhere in the upper gloom. It was a place where time had stood still, a place where there was nothing.

The matron whispered, "It's an awful place, isn't it? thank God, it will soon be gone", and then she added sadly, "I've seen young nurses break down and cry, when they walk across this floor".

Laura further deteriorated and was transferred to a hospital home for the terminally ill at Falmouth. Most of the time she spent sleeping, but at times would rouse herself, and talk for a little while to her new-found friends. They laughed together as she re-told her stories, the tarred window, and her friends the cats. She told them about her little two-roomed cottage on the edge of the village green, with the stream running alongside. Suddenly her eyes glazed, as if she was peering into another dimension, quietly she murmured to herself.

"It wus lov'ly there, 'specially in the summer, and wun day I'm gon back".

But she never did.

> For the needy shall not alway be forgotten;
> the expectation of the poor shall not perish forever.
> Psalm 9:18.

17

Regatta

Our local regatta was held in the Copperhouse Reach, usually referred to as Hayle Pool. It was entirely dependent on the very high tides, experienced in August and September. With the sluicing of the bar held in abeyance for twenty-four hours, the gates at "Bridge" were closed, trapping the high tide within, any leakage through the gates, would hopefully be compensated from the in-flowing river at the far Copperhouse end.

On a balmy day, it was a treat to sit on the Clifton Terrace bank, and watch the regatta, free of charge. Numerous collection boxes helped to top-up the ever-draining funds. If one had the money, for six-pence a seat could be purchased in the stand, a temporary structure of wooden frames near the bridge. The only advantage of sitting there, seemed to be a better view of the swimming races. We children couldn't afford such luxuries, and in any case, preferred to keep moving around.

Stalls were erected on the bend of the main road, by the "Pickle Jars", ice-cream, fudge, and toffee, were devoured in gargantuan quantities, (some people had more money than sense) Saw-dust balls wrapped in brightly coloured paper, whizzed and zapped the unwary behind the ear, returning quickly, via the elastic string, to the persecutor. The very young, contented themselves with something faintly resembling a bird, captive at the end of a string, and held by a wand. Spun around, the bird furiously beat its wings and tail, the whistle hidden in its beak, giving a pleasing trilling sound. The simplest and cheapest was the "Whizz-a-bout" simply two coloured celluloid propellors, revolving contrawise at the end of a stick! stirred into action by the breeze.

The "Bunco" boys were having a hey-day just outside the Customs House. Their little swindles all had a fixed price of six-pence. The magician certainly looked impressive, in his long purple costume and high pointed hat, all covered with mystical signs and stars. For only (you've guessed it) six-pence, your very own personal horoscope, via the magic crystal. The so-called magic crystal, appeared to us, as just a gold-fish bowl, but it mesmerised the crowd. Many parted with there hard earned tanner. For each participant the barker tore a sheet of blank paper from a writing pad, and dropped it in the crystal. With a flourish the bowl, (full of blank paper) was ceremoniously placed on a box, covered with a star decorated dark cloth. The onlookers went silent as the magician waved his wand, and muttered devious incantations. Lo! and behold! before their very eyes, the blank papers blossomed into writing. Quickly the barker retrieved the papers, handing them to the now thoroughly converted. The writing didn't last long, invisible ink has a habit of fading again, when out of its chemical environment.

I must admit I was fascinated by the watch trick. The unwary pushed forward, their gimlet eyes glued to the man putting numerous pocket-watches into many brown paper envelopes, and seal them. Into other packets he put worthless trinkets, usually found in halfpenny "lucky-bags". Everybody who took a chance, would get a prize, and as there seemed to be two or three times as many watches as there were junk packets, the chances of winning a time-piece, was positively with the investor.

"Now who will give me sixpence for this?"

The onlookers looked at the packet suspiciously, but no-one spoke. He joked, he pleaded, he inviegled, but there was no response.

"What a pity", he said, tearing the packet and taking out a watch. There were plenty of takers for the next packet, and many after that, but no-one was lucky enough to win the coveted prize. Realising they were being taken for a ride, the crowd started to drift away, then a shout went up.

"I've won a watch".

With the flame of greed once again ignited, they returned to their wily benefactor, but to no avail. Some had already paid for the watch, many times over, but at the time it never occurred to them, that the man who "won" the watch, was a plant. With the interest once again flagging, Bunco pointed to a bystander. "Go on, have a go, pick any envelope you wish". Sixpence lighter, the innocent pointed to an envelope. "I'll have that one". Bunco held the envelope high, for all to see.

"You are my witness, that this is the envelope he picked".

"No! No! I picked that other one".

"Not true, these people saw you pick this one".

"No we didn't".

"But I appeal to you to be fair".

"You don't appeal to us at all, give him the envelope he chose – or else".

Almost in tears, Bunco reluctantly handed over the envelope, the innocent eagerly tore it open, two glass beads fell into his out- stretched hand.

"Perhaps it would have been better if you chose the one I offered?" Bunco opened the packet, and extracted the elusive watch.

It was all very weird and wonderful to me, I was standing alongside the table, but still couldn't see how it was done. Of course there was only one watch, and that was in Bunco's pocket, it proved to be an expensive lesson to many, the only winner was the man behind the table.

With his audience now getting a bit ratty, Bunco quickly swept the remaining envelopes into an empty suitcase, and melted into the crowd.

All this time the regatta was in progress. We had some excellent swimmers in Hayle. George Gibson, from Cross Street, won many trophies. Leslie King was "King" of them all, he and his brothers practically monopolised the sport. Leslie was our champ', winning the County 1000, 440, 220, and 100 yard races. The fairer sex had their moments of glory, Tilly Thomas immediately springs to mind.

With a fair wind in the pool, the sailing races were a joy to watch, with the St Ives boats, like the "Ivor" dominating the scene, (much later, ownership of this boat passed to a Hayle resident). But the local enthusiasts had a card up their sleeve, the sailing boat's name was the "Coch a Bon Ddu", which translated was "Red Spider" or so the locals tell us, it was from the Welsh, the translation may not have been accurate, but suited Hayle very nicely. Brought down from "up-country" to meet the out-sider challengers. At first it was found to be too long, and only the free-for-all races were open. However, lopping two foot off the stern, solved the problem, the "Red Spider" sailed against all comers, and annihilated them.

Racing skiffs darted up and down the Pool. Donald Gunn, rowing the "Diamond", hailed from Truro river, a fine oarsman, and walked away with many "Firsts". Local competitor, Willie Love, battled gallantly behind the oars of the "Britannia", and enjoyed his share of triumphs. From Daniel's Shop, the "Lady Dorothy", contestant Dorothy Daniel herself, rowed in many regattas. "Dutchy" Hollow had a skiff especially built for his teen-age son, and young Jackie rowing the "Marigold", showed the older and more experienced contenders, how it should be done.

Naturally, the hydroplanes (they were speed-boats to us) thrilled young lads like myself most of all. We cheered as they bounced and skimmed, up and down the Pool in a shower of spray, the engines noisily roaring defiance at all and sundry, emblazoned on their hulls, the unforgettable legends, "Mississippi", "It's- It", and who could ever forget, "C-U-Later".

The bane of the regatta committee, was the nobbling of the boats, a practise difficult to detect, until too late, but the sheer inventiveness of the nobblers, afforded a great deal of amusement to the townsfolk.

The clinker built naval whalers, (salvaged from the breaker's yard) seemed to have been one of the prime targets, simply because they were the only boats left in the Pool, all the year around, and could be approached over dry land when the tide was out. I remember four of these boats, identical in appearance, except for the inch wide painted band, running around the gunnel, each boat with a different colour, Red, Blue, White and Yellow. Red and Blue were most favoured, they pulled fairly well, White was considered not quite as good. Yellow was to be avoided at all cost, for some unexplained reason, she yawed in all directions. Naturally the odds had to be evened out, and a little knobbling was called for. One year, "Red didn't behave at all, a post-mortem the next day at low tide, revealed lumps of old roofing lead, nailed just above the keel on the port side. The regatta committee waxed wrathfully at such desecration, much to the merriment of the populace. The simplest and most obvious way to knobble the whalers, was to alter the colour bandings. I can only remember this being tried once. Alas for the nobbler, he was caught with the brush and paint-pot, still in his hand. Righteous indignation from the committee, and more howls of laughter from the townsfolk.

Over the years, exposed as they were to the elements, the whalers slowly fell to pieces, not a vestige remains today.

The classic nobbling story, was a saga before my time, but I often heard it repeated around the fireside, and on the street corners.

Able was a very quiet, bluff sort of chap, in his mid' 60s, absolutely inpervious to the teasing and wise-cracking of his drinking companions. Joshua was ten years older, and with the exact opposite disposition, short in stature, and shorter in temper, blinking malevolently through his spectacles, defying all who disagreed with his exhalted opinions. They were, of course a ready-made vaudeville act for the "wags" who gathered at the "Pickle Jars". Every Saturday night it was the same script. After a few pints of "Ellis's" bitter, someone would drop the hint that Able was heard to say something derogatory about the little man. With the fuse well and truly lit, the explosion followed, arms were thrown around Joshua to prevent him from pulverising Able into the next world. "Outside, outside", he screamed, which in itself was quite hillarious, considering that Able was four stone the heavier. The quiet man never denied that he had said anything defamatory, simply looked at his pint, and pointed out, that he never used those exact words. This in itself was admission enough, to start the near riot all over again. So it was, the near fisticuffs of the two protagonists became a Saturday night feature, and the inventiveness of the "stirrers" almost unbelievable. Their real triumph was the "Challenge", and they proudly proclaimed it, "the best bit of stir-up, the town had ever witnessed".

Someone recalled that both Able and Joshua had, in their youth, rowed in the regatta, each with some moderate success. It didn't take the wags long to turn the conversation towards this volatile subject, and they argued for some time, who was the better man?. Finally they decided, after examining all the evidence, gleaned from the reminiscence of the older factions, that without doubt, Able must have been that man. No sooner was the bait dangled, than it was snapped up, hook, line, and sinker.

"Better than me was 'e?" the little man shrieked, "I could lick the a . . . off him anytime, all wind and p . . . thats w'ot 'e is". Able looked down at the bundle of seething fury,

"Josh' boy, you couldn't lick me then, and certainly couldn't do it now".

"Is that so? Is that so? just because I'm a few years older, you think I'm easy meat, well, we'll see about that, let us see you put your money where your mouth is. I challenge you Able Big Mouth, to a rowing contest in the regatta, just you and me".

Able nodded in agreement, and continued drinking, the die was cast and the plotters very happy. Everything had turned out as they had planned, to the very letter.

The great day arrived, the story of the challenge spread like wild-fire through the town, and all waited impatiently for the promised event.

At last, over the megaphone, the long awaited announcement.

"Ladies and Gentlemen, as an extra to our programme, a special challenge, single oar, skiff race, between our old friends, Able an Joshua. The winner will receive a grand prize of thirty shillings".

Amid some titters and applause, both contestants walked to the waters edge. Able clambered into his skiff, and pulled towards the starting line. Joshua started, as a voice from a rowing boat called to him, "Come on, jump in", bewildered he accepted the invitation, "Eh! what's happened to my boat?"

"Don't worry", replied the voice, "it's already at the starting line, I'll row you out to it, it'll save your strength, give you a bit of an edge". Joshua kept quiet, there was some wisdom in those words, the ten years difference in age, was more than a bit of a disadvantage.

With both contestants more or less safely seated in their craft, they waited, under starters orders.

"Get ready" – "Go" – The starter's gun barked, and a shower of No. 6. shot sped across the Pool, falling as lead rain on the unsuspecting Town Band, who were playing the "Eton Boating Song" for the umpteenth time. (It was an "accident" that seemed to occur at regular painful intervals, during our regattas).

Able gave a strong pull on the oars, the skiff leapt away from the starting line. The years dropped away, it was like the old times all over again, only this time there was no serious competition. He suddenly realised that Joshua was no longer alongside, and he hadn't passed. Looking back, he saw the older man moving very slowly away from the starting line.

Things hadn't gone too well for Joshua. At the sound of the gun, he had given a tremendous pull on the oars, but nothing had happened, except that his arms had almost popped out of their sockets. At first it occurred to him that he had fouled some underwater obstacle, but a hurried glance around, revealed nothing. He settled back once again, this time pulling a little steadier, sure enough the skiff very slowly moved away. "My Gawd", he wheezed, "can't ever remember these boats being this heavy, probably be alright when I get my second wind". Twenty yards down the course, Able waited until the other skiff came alongside.

"You alright Josh'?"

"Course I'm alright, bit out of practice thats all". And so it went on, Able pulling ahead, then waiting for Joshua to catch him up. By the time they had reached the far end of the Pool, circled the marker buoy, and started back, Able was getting very worried. The old man was in a near-collapsed condition, but pig-headed, still struggling with the oars, his face flushed like a blood-pit.

"Let's give up", suggested Able.

"Never", panted the old man.

"Face the fact, your boat's been got at".

"Nothing wrong with my boat, I've checked, if you've had enough why don't you pack up?"

It was no use trying to talk to a brick wall, so Able contented himself by rowing alongside. Both boats reached the finishing- line at the same time, he looked anxiously at Joshua, flaked out and prostrate, a rescue boat already on its way to take him in.

By the time of prize-giving, an hour later, Josh' had made a remarkable recovery, and was once again his old irascible self.

The marquee was crammed with supporters, the "wags" filling the first three rows. At last it was time for the "Challenge Prize", "It has been decided by the committee", said the chairman, "that because of the closeness of the finish, the prize-money will be equally divided between our two sporting contestants. Shouts of "Hear hear", from the audience. Able's name was read out, and he sheepishly moved to the presentation table, and accepted his 15/-, amid the loud "boohs" from the rows of grinning faces.

Joshua was then called to the front, and presented with his prize-money. Loud and long the cheers echoed through the marquee, but as far as the old man was concerned, there was far too much frivolity for such an auspicious occasion. He glared them to silence, drew himself up to his full five-foot-four, and with as much dignity as he could muster, delivered his carefully prepared short speech.

"It was a tough race", he began, (titters and "quiet please" rippled around the tent) "but I wish to admit, here and now, that Able was the better man, I am of course ten years older than he, but let's face the fact, I almost beat the s.. didn't I?"

Joshua didn't get any further, the marquee almost collapsed with the uproar, it was something that puzzled him, for the rest of his life, and he never again spoke to Danny Polsue, who laughed so much, that he suddenly fell down, in what appeared to be, an apoplectic fit, and was carried outside to recover.

In the meantime, two swimmers swam to the skiff, still moored near the finishing line. One clambered aboard, and untied the mooring, the other dived underneath, and with a deft stroke of a knife, severed a rope nailed to the keel.

The rope with a large bucket suspended at the other end, fell away silently, to the sandy bottom.

Today their real names may be forgotten, but their story will forever linger on.

The tales of Hayle Regatta, could never be complete, without some reference to the town's most celebrated yachtsman.

Hughie was the man who wouldn't give up. He loved boats, for him the annual regatta was the highlight of the year. He was the proud possessor of a sailing boat, the G.W.B. (named after his nephew, Graham Wilson Barrett). Unfortunately the hull was as "rotten-as-a-pear", her sails resembled a dark grey patchwork quilt, under constant threat of disintegration. Stories about him are legend. There was the time he ventured forth into St Ives Bay, with a contingent of gullible tourists, when one of his passengers put his foot through the lower planks, and they struggled back to harbour refuge, all sitting along one side, in an endeavour to keep the gaping hole clear of the "drink".

Never daunted, Hughie always believed that one day he would win the "Town Cup", an optimism born from frustration and futile hope. With the boat pulled up on dry land, alongside the Baptist Church, he spent many, many hours preparing the G.W.B. for the great day. At times his nephews, Graham and Peter, went along to help him, although they knew, the old boat could never be a serious competitor. Every year he entered, and every year it was the same story, he came in last. Always the optimist, he would shrug his shoulders and say, "With a bit of luck I'll win next year".

The listeners moved away to hide their smiles.

It was a beautiful balmy Saturday for the regatta, with the water very calm. This was ideal for the swimmers and rowers, but not so good for the yachtsmen. However, the sailing races did progress at a very leisurely pace. The mile long pool was, more or less, landlocked, anxious eyes turned skywards, a further drop in the wind would court disaster.

Finally the yachts lined up for the "Town Cup", the G.W.B. sticking out like a sore thumb, in the midst of the pristine collection of brightly coloured hulls and snow-white sails. A loud blast from the starters shotgun, and they were – Off – all except Hughie, who was experiencing a little difficulty in getting away, it obviously was not going to be his day.

With the competitors at least 100 yards down the Pool, Hughie, still

H. T. Love
(photo: C. Thomas)

at the starting line, witnessed an unbelievable scene. The wind dropped suddenly away, and the proud craft, reduced to limp sails and practically rudderless, bumped and jostled each other uncontrollably. For twenty minutes they tried to sort out the mayhem, but to no avail. Shouts and curses rang down the Pool, crews were jumping into the water, in an effort to pull their battered craft out of harms way. The larger boats from St Ives, found themselves with another problem. Overnight the dock gates had leaked badly, and the depth of the water decreased alarmingly. These boats suddenly found their keels stuck to the mud on the bottom. There was only one thing to do, down with the sails, up with the drop-keel, and row out of trouble. Eventually all the boats were pulled to the safety of the shore line, except the G.W.B. "After all", Hughie reasoned, "he hadn't put in all those hours of work, only to be deprived of his two laps on regatta day, regardless of the fact that the Town Cup Race, would now be abandoned!. So he slowly drifted past the carnage, dreamily hypnotised by the sagging languid sails.

How he managed those two laps, nobody ever knew, at one time he picked up a couple of passengers, but they soon tired of seemingly going nowhere, and with muttered curses, jumped into the shallows, and waded ashore.

It was evening by the time Hughie finished the course, and tied the G.W.B. to a stone by "Clodgey Bay". He walked up the bank and looked around, the Pool was deserted. It was obvious where everybody had gone, the sound of the silver band, leading the Town Carnival, resounded clearly across the water.

He walked to the awning of the presentation marquee, and peered inside. The wooden folding chairs and tables were already stacked for collection the next morning. Excepting, that is, for one card table, at the far end of the tent, and on that table, the coveted "Town Cup". He stepped into the stillness, and walked the length of the marquee, to the table, looked longingly at the silver cup, which he knew could never be his, touched the rim and murmured to himself, "Perhaps, next year".

There was a red card inside the cup, he picked it up, and in the fading light, read the inscription.

Hayle Regatta Committee.

Town Cup.

FIRST

Hugh Thomas Love.

I have never heard that Hughie could swim, but then, few local seamen could. They voiced the opinion, that the time to learn was when they found themselves in the drink. Many times Hughie tempted providence, and the "Pearly Gates" beckoned, but someone "up there" must have liked him. His most celebrated brush with the hereafter, was when he was working as boat-man in the harbour, November 1934.

The steamship S.S.Taycraig (a small coaster of 163 tons) steamed into Hayle harbour with a cargo of coal from Wales. It was usual to turn the ship around on the anchor, either coming in or going out, ready for, "across the bar, and outward bound". Unbelievingly, Hughies rowing boat was under the anchor when it dropped. The ton or more of anchor and chain, reduced the wooden row-boat to a flotsam of matchwood. Twice he disappeared beneath the briny, and twice he climbed the anchor chain before finally being pulled to safety by the Taycraig's crew. Except for shock, he suffered little physical injury.

Fourteen months later,' January 1936, the Taycraig floundered on "Gear Rock", during a storm in Mounts Bay. At least two Hayle men were crew members on that ill-fated ship, Harry Richardson from Market Street, was the fireman, and another chap by the name of Gilbert was on the bridge at the time. Fortunately both survived their ordeal.

Sadly Hughie ended his days, a helpless invalid, with both his legs amputated. The G.W.B. had fallen to pieces some decades before.

For tho' from out our bourne of time and place
The flood may bear me far
I hope to see my Pilot face to face
When I have crost the bar.

A. Tennyson 1809–1892.
(Pub' 1889)

18

Wreckers

I suppose there will always be smuggling, whenever the opportunity presents itself, but by the mid' 19th century, the romantic storybook smuggler, operating from sailing ships and landing contraband on a moonlit beach, had passed into history. Smuggling had reduced itself to a few ankers of brandy, hidden with the legitimate cargo. The local Vicar imbibed the expensive French spirit, and asked no questions, after all, it was a traditional way of life. The old men sat in the "Kiddleys" and retold their smuggling adventures over and over again.

Many stories have been told and written about the Cornish smuggler, much of it fiction, but there is very little said about the "Wrecker".

The word "Wrecker", is a description loosely applied to a number of different dubious occupations. Immediately springs to mind, a mental image of lanterns hanging from donkeys, enticing some off-course ship, battling in a storm, to a supposedly safe refuge, only to find, too late, that there is no sanctuary, nothing but the sound of rocks tearing the ship's bottom asunder, and the anguished cries of the terror stricken crew. Any that survived were put to the sword, No witnesses, no questions.

The stories still persist today, and there is little doubt, that it happened. However these wreckers would hardly be foolish enough to leave behind much documentary evidence. Watching a ship disintegrate on the rocks, during a storm, and then plunder the cargo, at considerable risk to their own lives, was a risk born of idiocy. Far better to lure the vessel to a sheltered cove, safely beached, it was an easy prey.

As for the untimely despatch of the crew members, I'll let my grandmother Eliza Philp, tell her story.

"When I was not yet three years old, I stood on the beach during a storm, and watched the ship-wrecked sailors swim to the shore, The young men of the village lined the edge of the water, armed with boat

89

oars. As the survivers came out of the surf, their heads were 'stoved' in, and the lifeless bodies pushed back into the water".

I questioned her story, "Could it be that the oars were used for reaching out, and so help bring the sailors to the shore?"

She paused, looked at me and said, "I know what I saw".

I asked her if she thought the ship had been deliberately wrecked.

She replied, "I don't know, I was so young at the time, and wouldn't have understood, even if I had been told".

I was only a schoolboy when I first heard this story, but my father, uncles and aunts, repeated it many times in the following years. I often wonder where it could have happened. She was born at Illogan, the nearest beach would be Portreath, so I reasoned it must have been there, or some other beach near-by.

The story is still told in family circles, and is now part of our family history.

Another of her recollections, concerned, what must have been, the last of the naval Press Gangs. Whenever a warship hove into view, her brothers hid themselves down a disused mine shaft. Every day the little girl toddled along to the shaft, and lowered a food parcel on the end of a string, to her beleaguered kin-folk. No- one took any notice of the little girl, least of all, the navy. She did this until the ship finally up-anchored, sailed away, and her brothers re-emerged into the sunlight.

Other "Wreckers" were the pilferers, they kept their eyes open and peeled, after every storm, for any doomed ship driven ashore.

The tale of the Pendeen wreck raised a few chuckles.

Late, one moonlit night, during a half-gale, a steam freighter rammed herself on the rocks, near Pendeen. From the bridge, the captain spotted, what appeared to be, a pathway up the cliff face. He made an on-the-spot decision. Two Lascars were to be left behind, as a deterent against would-be salvage claims. The freighter was in no immediate danger of breaking up, the two Lascars would be safe until help arrived.

The captain and the rest of the crew made their way up the cliff-path, and walked into Pendeen to raise the alarm. The good people of that village quickly found food and shelter for the ship- wrecked mariners, but seemed little interested in the wreck, it wasn't going anywhere, and would still be there in the morning.

But on the ship a scary drama was unfolding, with the lascars staring pop-eyed over the ships rail. Down the cliff-path came a procession of silent ghostly figures, armed with crowbars, axes, saws, and other implements of impending destruction, the weak light reflecting from their candle lanterns, gave the scene a spectrality that frightened the living daylights out of the watchers. Shaking with fear, they fled to the stern of the ship, squeezed themselves into a locker, jammed the door on the inside, and prayed to their God.

The Wreckers were very thorough, and seldom spoke to each other, obviously they had done it all before. Then just at day-break – silence – The frightened seamen finally plucked up the courage to venture out of their self-imposed confinement, just in time to see the Captain and some coastguards negotiating the cliff-path back to the ship.

Everything removable, including the ships wheel and binnacle, had been spirited away, the once proud vessel, looked as though she had sailed through a typhoon.

"We know who they are", wept a coastguard, "they won't get away with it this time". And so an immediate investigation was mounted. For the next few days, houses, barns, fields and byways, were diligently searched, in an endeavour to locate the missing loot, and one must admit they had some small measure of success, a dinner-plate –

The felon was hauled into court, the magistrate giving the unfortunate a deservedly good dressing down, pointed out the error of his ways, and then with a twinkle in his eye, fined him ten-bob.

The term "Wrecker", is (in some books) loosely applied to the beach-comber, but to me this is a contradiction of terms. Men out of work, walked up and down the beach, hoping they might find something of use, not my definition of Wreckers.

In 1936 the "Bessemer City" floundered on the rocks at Pen Enys Point, and some of her cargo of tinned fruit, salmon, etc, drifted on to the sands at Hayle. Unfortunately tin-plate offers little protection against the salt water, and most of the salvage was contaminated and uneatable. However careful selection did result in some tins being found in a good condition, and families, too poor to buy such luxuries, suddenly found their kitchen wall cupboards, well stocked.

A better find was the box of sultanas that Tom Crewes found in the surf near the bar. These he took home to Ventonleague. Still in the wooden box, the dried fruit were left for some time in the stream, to wash away the salt, and then dried in the sun. Cake instead of just bread, for the next few weeks.

In 1938 the Italian collier "Alba" wrecked herself on the rocks of St

Ives Island, and some of its cargo found its way to our beach. The loot was gathered up into sacks, and wheelbarrowed away.

The powers-that-be didn't bother to investigate, there was no duty owing, and after all, one piece of coal looks much like the other.

Our family seldom benefitted from these findings. Father frowned on beach-combing, although I noticed that anything useful he "stumbled" across, found its way to our home. I would have loved to have gone myself, but my mother shook her head in disapproval, and her word was law.

In 1937, there was a wreck we all had an interest in, practically every one I knew had their share of the spoils.

A French vessel with a cargo of wine, floundered off Guernsey. Many large casks survived the long journey from the Channel Isles to the Cornish coast. From Mullion, around Lands End, to Portreath and beyond, these large casks drifted ashore. St Ives Bay was dotted with them, with many destined for Hayle beach.

Uncle Dick was rabbiting near the cliff top, and was probably the first local to sight them.

He said, "I heard a bumping noise, and walked down to the beach to investigate. In the bright moonlight I saw them, huge barrels coming ashore everywhere. They were too large for me to handle, then I spotted two small ankers against the rocks, I waded into the water, and retrieved them. An hour later they were safely stored away in my shelter on the Army firing range".

The kegs that Dick found, contained white wine, and this proved to be a better find than the more prolific red.

At that time we had moved from St John's Street, to near-by Cornubia Hill, and it was from a vantage point in the Front-room window, that I watched the opportunists returning from the beach with their spoils. Anything that could hold liquid was utilised, bottles, buckets, and even galvanised baths, were brought into play. I watched fascinated as they struggled and toiled homeward.

On the beach bedlam had broken loose, this time the coastguards had an interest, no duty had been paid on the wine, therefore the casks were to be broken, and the wine allowed to drain away. Proving without fear of contradiction, that "the law is an ass". The too few coastguards, ran up and down the long beach, like Keystone Cops, puncturing the casks with small axes. All in vain, someone would come along, plug the hole with seaweed (or whatever) and then calmly open another hole nearer the top and drain off his bucket or bathful, leaving ample for the next. One man and his son dragged a large bathful over the sand dunes, only to find His Majesties Rep' waiting for them, curtly he ordered the wine to be tipped, but as soon as his back was turned, they went back to the beach and replenished the tub. My cousin, Robert Philp, managed to get astride of a barrel, in an attempt to prevent it being washed back out to sea, he would probably have been swept into the obituary columns, if someone hadn't thrown him a rope. For many months to come, Hayle was awash with wine, it tasted awful, obviously it hadn't matured, and in all probability was to have been used in blending. Allowing it to mature over a period of time, didn't seem to improve the taste. Many years later, I often saw cobwebbed bottles still on shelves, at the back of coal houses. A momento of Cornwall's glorious (or inglorious) past.

We only stayed a year on Cornubia Hill, mother never liked it there. By the end of 1938, we were back in our old house, in St John's Street.

Finally there was the Wrecker-Captain, who conveniently lost his ship for the insurance.

The stories were handed down by the ancients, who gathered in the kitchen, and sat there all the evening, spinning fascinating sea- going yarns to each other.

A single-burner oil lamp on the table, set the scene.

(A) "Remember the ole S.S. ——?"

(B) "Did a good job with 'er we did, a bit foggy at the time, but the sae was nice an' kalm".

(A) "Odd 'ow it 'appened, you boys knawing the coast as you did".

(B) "Nothin' odd 'bout it, all carefully planned boy. Ole 'Jam Jars' was on watch, 'e never could see beyon' 'is nawse", then as an afterthought, "bl . . . . ole tub, falling apart anyhow".

(A) "You're lucky she went on the rocks, just where it was nice and easy to git to the top of the cliff and the road".

(B) (In mock exasperation) "Stands to reason, we picked a spot where there was little danger, and the road 'ad to be nearby so that we poor shipwrecked sailors could get a lift 'ome, 'eroes that's what we were".

(A) "Did they ever give 'e a backhander?"

(B) "Not a bl . . . . penny".

(A) "Mean ole s . . . , perhaps they thought you 'adn't caught on?"

(B) "They nod alright, and they nod that if we opened our mouths, 'ell would break loose. All my working days I found them more than a bit cadgy".

(A) "How d'ye mean?"

(B) "Well .... when I was out of work, all I 'ad to do was turn up at their office and say, in a loud voice, 'I was on the S.S.———'. They would look at me for a minute, and then tell me to report fer the next sailing. Full employment fer the rest of my life, that was my backhander boy".

They chatted away as if I wasn't there, and it only registered to me, a small child, as just another interesting story. Their faces are blurred by the passing time, but their voices I can still hear.

"Dear Lord, we hope that there will be no
shipwrecks, but if there be, let them be
at St Just for the benefit of the inhabitants".
Pulpit prayer, attributed to Parson Amos Mason 1650.
(but with slight variations in other parts of Cornwall,
and the Isles of Scilly).

19

The Seafarers

Like most harbours around Cornwall, Portreath, during the nineteenth century, built a few small ships. In 1867 Thomas Massey began building ocean-going sailing ships. The first of the line was a wooden hull, two mast, top-sail schooner, with a gross tonnage of 128 tons.

My great-grandfather took the "Bessie Belle" from the stocks as her first captain. Although still in his early twenties, he was always referred to as "the old man", a title given to most sea captains at that time. I remember seeing one of those head and shoulder portraits, photographed after retirement. A flat unsmiling face, with a broken nose, set off by a round seaman's beard, stared at me with baleful menace. He was said to be "short of stature, short of temper", anyone on ship attempting to usurp his authority, found themselves on the wrong end of a belaying-pin and suffering a cracked skull. His reputation was so bad, that few would venture to sea with him, and most of those who did, lived to regret it. No one had a good word for him, he was referred to by the polite, as a "devil incarnate", and dismissed by the impolite, with colourful expletives.

When the son, Jim, informed his mother of his intention to serve under the "Old man", she begged him to reconsider, "He'll murder you", she prophesied.

Jim sailed with his father for two years, and got along quite well with the reprobate. An argument finally put an end to the union, Jim did not relish the thought of being laid flat out on the deck, with a sore head. It was time to move on to more congenial pastures.

The "Old man" struck up a friendship with three drop-outs from the village, it was a question of "birds of a feather".

The days of smuggling on a grandiose scale, had long passed, but ships to the continent, often returned with a few ankers of Brandy. Old ways die hard, and Brandy was the ideal contraband, being almost imperishable. The pubs enjoyed the influx of the illicit cargo, the village

'Bessie Bell'. 1903
(photo: Morwellham Quay

Jim Philp, my Great Uncle
(photo: R. Davey)

policeman was not forgotten, with two bottles of the "very best" left on his doorstep. Portreath's custodian of the law was rather exceptional, he spent the whole of his police career in that village, and never had a case. Boisterous youths were firmly put in their place, by a quick boot up the backside. Drunks were escorted home, and as for the petty smuggling, – well – that was the coastguards' problem.

With a few ankers retained for their own personal use, the "Fiercesome four" decided to cache them, in their usual hide-a- way. This was a cave, in the cliff face just off Portreath, very difficult to locate, and approachable only from the sea. Huge boulders falling from the cliff face, had further obscured the entrance. Their get-togethers were few and far and far between, but when the opportunity arose, they assembled on the quayside, hopped into a boat, rowed to the cave, and soon were roaring drunk. Then in an alchoholic daze manoeuvered the boat back to the village, to the best of their now diminished prowess. Struggling back to the quay, collapsing into an untidy heap, to sleep it off wherever they lay. On one occasion, all did not go quite according to plan. The "Old man" aroused himself with a daddy of a hangover, only to find one of their number missing. "Anyone seed Hezzie?" but nobody had, and then with the wisdom of Solomon he added, "Bl . . . . ole fool must 'ave fallen overboard, no use looking for 'im now". They all agreed, and without further ado, went their respective ways.

The disappearance of Hezzie raised little interest in the village, he was a "fariner", an outsider, and so was quickly forgotten. When the constable questioned the "Old man", he simply replied that he had no idea where 'ezzie could be, then with a malicious grin added, "I think 'e be gon bak to sae". At that point, the constable gave up, realising, that, that was as near to the truth as he was ever likely to get.

The son, Jim Philp, lived out his retirement years in a small house in Bodriggy Street, Hayle. Like many of the old seamen, he was a splendid raconteur, his favourite story, without a doubt, was, "The Cannon". I heard him tell it many times, and can remember it in detail.

A Naval Cutter had come to grief on the rocks off Portreath. Viewed by the villagers, from an advantage point on Battery Hill, it seemed a prime catch indeed. Normally a few hours would suffice to reduce such a vessel to a skeletal ruin, but the Navy, fully aware of the plundering habits of the Cornish, mounted armed guards along the cliff tops, a pretentiousness soon to be doomed to ignominious failure.

The "Old Man" gazed at the distant ship, with some apprehension,

97

it only needed half-a-gale and his rightful inheritance would disintegrate into matchwood, all that lovely loot would never see the light of day again. The "Fiercesome Four" (now reduced to the "Terrible Three) held a hasty conference, and a plan of action decided on.

A few nights later, the sea was still, with the moon conveniently curtained by heavy clouds. (The Devil looks after his own). Muffled oars silently propelled a row-boat from the far end of the beach. Cautiously it nosed its way along the coast, making a long detour, before finally coming around to the seaward side of the Cutter, hopefully hidden from the prying eyes of the watchers on the cliff.

Less than an hour after leaving the shore, three furious sailors stood on the deck of the doomed vessel, staring in disbelief at the carnage about them. Everything that could be moved, had been taken, the furniture, tables, chairs, pots, pans, and of course, as always, the ships wheel and binnacle. It was a ship without sails, ropes, bedding or victuals. The "Old man" was near to tears, "Them s . . . from Porthtowan 'ave bin 'ere", he wailed. They were just about to return to their boat, when he spotted it – a small signal cannon. These little guns were often used by the Navy for firing blank charges, but were capable of firing small cannon balls. The cast-iron barrel was mounted on a solid wooden block, without wheels, and pulled around on the deck by means of a rope. At least it was something to save face. Carefully they lowered their prize into the boat, and returned to the harbour by their already proven circuitous route.

The next day, their newly acquired toy was proudly on display, near the galley of the "Bessie Belle", and the cook promoted to "Chief Cannonier".

There was a number of very good reasons for this.

The cook was considered the lowest form of animal life, and cooked only for the captain, (the crew brought their own cold pasties and sandwiches, although a cup of hot tea was always on hand). He was invested with a number of duties, that had nothing to do with culinary expertise, such as cleaning out the Captain's cabin. The "Bessie Belle" was a very fast schooner, and given a fair following wind, could easily overtake the "Steam Kettles" (tramp steamers) of that time. It was the cook's prerogative to wave his mop, over the stern rail, at the receding steam ship, a sort of sailors farewell, or to put it more crudely, "Kiss my —", a gesture not at all appreciated by the "Kettle" captains.

The mop handle could now be further utilised for tamping down the powder and ball of the cannon. The powder had been easily obtainable, and one of the crew retrieved a number of small cannon balls from the bottom of his garden, which miraculously were the right size. The cook was also the only custodian of a red hot poker, essential for the firing of a gun from the wind swept deck of a sailing ship. On rest periods, members of the crew often amused themselves by discharging the cannon at anything, in the water, that moved, but never scoring a hit. The marksmen soon tired of watching the iron balls bounce across the water, and with powder and shot fast dwindling, the "Old man" decreed, that in future, the gun would only be fired at his command.

And so, Captain Philp became the only skipper on the coast, in command of an armed merchantman, it only needed a Skull and cross-bones at the mast head, to complete the picture. Whenever the "Bessie Belle" approached harbour, there would be a flash and a roar, as the little cannon bucked under the recoil.

"Let 'em knaw we're commin' ", grinned the "Old man". The inhabitants of the port, crossed themselves, looked at each other, and said, "Oh gawd ees back agin".

One day while sailing along the coast, the Captain with his eagle eye glued to the scope, saw a movement in the fast approaching Perranporth sands. A young couple, unaware of being watched, were gratifying their carnal lust, with amorous passion.

"Bring 'er in as close as 'e can".

The wheel turned and the schooner sailed on gracefully, just clear of the breaking surf.

"Load the cannon".

The cook yanked the gun sideways by means of a rope, pulled the wood plug from the muzzle, poured in the powder, and tamped it down with the mop handle. Next, a torn crumpled page of the "West Briton" was rammed home, then came the ball, and more paper, finally the lead apron over the "Touch" was removed, and a little powder trickled into the small hole. In less than half-a-minute, the cannon was pointing wickedly across the water, – primed and ready – The cook retreated to the galley, to await further orders.

The captain bided his time until the "Bessie Belle" was almost opposite the unsuspecting couple.

"Poker", he bellowed.

The cook reappeared, brandishing the red-hot iron, – and then froze.

"You're bl . . . mad, you are, I'm not firing that thing at them".

"Giv' it 'ere", the captain grabbed at the poker, and stabbed at the touch-hole, there was a loud explosion, voluminous black smoke blew across the deck.

As Jim was an eye-witness, I'll let him finish the story.

"It was a good shot, the ball struck the sand just below, and about six feet to the left of the target. It skidded up the bank scattering sand in all directions, and showering over the terrified couple". Jim paused at this point, then with a twinkle in his eye, he added, "The last we saw of them, they were running hell-for-leather up the sand dunes, and she had her knickers in her hand, I'll never forget it, we laughed all the way to Newport".

I didn't ask him, what might have happened if the shot had been a little more accurate, I had an uneasy feeling, that, that, might have spoiled the story.

When the "Old Man" retired from the sea, he took a job (of all things) as preventive officer, for the coastguards. One of the props of office, was a naval cutlass, still in the family today. It was a vocation, he considered himself admirably suited for, and with his bottle of French brandy constantly being replenished, there was little to report, to the satisfaction of all.

But old age finally took its toll, and his last years were spent in a cottage at Portreath, with his two unmarried daughters, one of them worked in the village shop. The little cannon remained with him, and had pride-of-place in the garden, the cast iron barrel regularly rust-proofed with generous rubbings of black lead.

When he died, he was buried in the churchyard at Illogan, I remember my father cycling off to Portreath, to attend the funeral, a distance of some ten miles. I have never found his tombstone, and there is no one alive today, to remind me of his christian names. He is always referred to, as the old captain, or the "Old man".

The cannon remained, like a memorial, in the garden, but in the late 1930's the wood supporting carriage succumbed to the elements. Never daunting, the daughters employed a local carpenter, to build another, and so it stayed with them, until they too passed on.

As for the Bessie Belle' she was last seen, in the 1920's, near Saltash, with her masts cut down, reduced to a nameless "Coal hulk". And there with her keel firmly embedded in the mud of the Tamar, she slowly rotted into oblivion.

"No mercy plea; no quarter given,
no favour sought; from man or Heaven"

D.P. 1990.

The "convict", was another saga from Jim, and another forgotten name, so I'll just call him Isaac Philp. Like his brother the "Old man", he answered the call of the sea. While still a young man, he was successful enough to purchase a half share in a schooner, trading around the coast, with the occasional voyage to Ireland and the Continent.

It was when the ship was docked at Truro, that Isaac received some very disquieting news, via the sailor's grape-vine.

In his absence, his partner had been preparing the ship for a long voyage. It was obvious to the dockers and sailors that the schooner was soon to be spirited away, to some distant land, and never to return. A valuable ship would be quite an asset to the setting up of a new life in the Americas. Infuriated by this treachery, Isaac purchased a keg of gunpowder, carried it to the dockside, and cached it in the hold of the ship.

The roar of the explosion could be heard over all Truro, the ship's bottom split assunder, by the time a crowd had gathered, the shattered vessel was lying under the waves, with only her masts showing above the water. Unfortunately for all concerned, the wreck had now effectively blocked part of the harbour.

There was no doubt who perpetrated the crime, the many clues pointed only to one person, Isaac. He was arrested and tried at the Falmouth court, the verdict was a forgone conclusion, he was to be taken in chains to a prison hulk at Gosport, and there he would languish, until a ship transported him to "Van Diemen's Land", usually a journey of no return.

There is no account of his eight month voyage, to the earth's farthest corner, Isaac made no reference to the deprivation, the crowding, the reeking stench, he must have endured while chained in the bowels of a ship. Perhaps he just wanted to forget it.

He finally arrived at his destination, and was incarcerated in the notorious penal prison at Hobart. Yet again, information about his captivity in that hell-hole, was a story never passed down, but the history of Hobart's Victorian horror, has been well documented in other authorative tomes.

We do know, that after a time he was allowed to join a working party,

101

on a farm not far from the town, but Isaac had other aspirations, and being an unpaid farmworker was not one of them. He saw his opportunity, and affected an escape. Hiding out until dark, and then moving stealthily into Hobart's dockland, making discreet enquiries at the many taverns. In one of these establishments of ill-repute, he soon found the sympathetic ear of some west-country seamen. Before the dawn broke, he was safely stowed away on a Barque, bound for "Blighty".

On such a long voyage it is inconceivable that the ships captain knew nothing of the stowaway, so under his unseeing eye, Isaac worked his passage homewar, as an unpaid nonentity. The Barque finally docked in the river Thames, many long and terrible years, after he had departed from Gosport, as a chained convict.

The Captain must have relented somewhat regarding the wages, for Isaac walked down the gangplank, with a fair sum of money in his pocket, and headed for the West Country. He stayed for a day near Padstow, renewing old family friendships, then moved on to Portreath, to see his brother Captain Philp, (the Old Man).

Although Jim was only a very young lad at the time, he never forgot the coming of his uncle, which isn't surprising, he had never seen a man dressed in woman's clothing before. The disguise must have been effective, the custodian of the law was noticeable by his absence. The two brother Captains sat in the kitchen, chattting long into the small hours.

It was too dangerous to stay more than one night, the next day Isaac said his goodbyes and walked from the village.

Two years later, the "Old man" received a letter, with a London post mark.

> "I'm doing very nicely, married and
> settled down. We have a little fish
> shop, and trade is good".

It was unsigned, and there was no address.

Somewhere in the archives of 19th century Cornish newspapers, there is a story about an explosion on a schooner at Truro, and the consequent arrest of the felon responsible. Overwhelmed with convicts, transportation to Van Diemen's Land was suspended in 1853. The Penal Station at Hobart closed in 1867, somewhere along these dates lie the rest of the story. I have taken the liberty of using "ship" to refer to a number of different vessels, but the old sailors only used the term, when talking about a sailing vessel, with 3 masts, with tops and yards to each. Jim never mentioned Tasmania, to him it was "Van Diemen's Land".

More than half-a-century later, Jim visited Hobart and looked at the old derelict prison, he tried to imagine how the convicts lived and died in such a place, but their cries of pain and anguish, could no longer be heard, only the chorus of the nesting birds. Still, Jim was glad he had seen the prison where his uncle had been incarcerated, a little bit of family history had at last been recorded in his memory, and finalised.

A brother of Jims was William Henry Philp, Queen Victoria (that bitter ole weed) was on the throne when W.H.P received his first captaincy.

I only remember seeing him once, in 1928, at his home in Mount Pleasant, Hayle. My father had taken me along with him, when on a Sunday morning visit. I stared in some trepidation at the stocky figure, with a bristling moustash, sitting in the gloom of the kitchen, soaking his feet in a tub of hot water. To bathe his feet in hot soapy water, each and every day, was a ritual he rigorously adhered to, all his life, on land or at sea. He claimed it was the best antidote for colds, influenza, and realitive illnesses. True, there is no record of him every suffering from these common ailments.

He looked at me with little curiosity, and spoke but a few words, I had a feeling that I was making no lasting impression. I stammered a hesitant reply, even as an old man he still exuded a strange hypnotic power of authority. Although not yet four years old, I sensed that the Captain was not one to be trifled with. I never saw him again, but I'm glad I was given the opportunity of seeing the grandfather, I had heard so much about, just that once.

As far as I know, he only captained two ships. The first was the S.S.Ailsa (scottish for Elsie) a steam coaster. Most of his working life was spent on the Bridge of that little ship.

He left his home at Portreath, sometime in the latter half of the nineteenth century, after marrying Eliza Webber from nearby Illogan, where she worked in service, as a domestic, to a large residence. No doubt Eliza was glad to rid herself of the drudgery of a live-in full time job, for just a few shillings per year, with, of course, the obligatory one day annual holiday. Married at Illogan Church, they moved to Hayle and set up home at Mount Pleasant. William Henry had been approached

Cap'n W. H. Philp. With daughters Emma (left) and Flo'
(photo: R. Davey)

by the ship owners "Williams of Scorrier", and offered the captaincy of the "Ailsa". It was usual to promote the ships masters from the lower ranks, if they appeared to have the accepted qualities for command. His salary of two pounds per week, sounds ridiculously low by today's standards, but at that time it represented more than twice what he could earn on land.

Eleven children were born at Mount Pleasant, seven boys and four girls, sadly one little girl died of meningitis, she was only months old, the iron cross marking Winifred's last resting place, can still be seen in Phillack Church Yard, and dated July 17, 1898.

With the captain spending most of his life at sea, the seven boys ran amuck, their rougish exploits would easily fill a book.

The Copperhouse Wesleyan Day School, like all the other schools of the nineteenth and early twentieth centuries, was ruled with a rod of iron, or rather with a number of corporal punishment instruments, ranging from the stinging ashplant, to the frightening flogging cane. Under the eagle eye of headmaster Thomas Jolly Porter, discipline was very harsh, with painful wallopings frequently dished out to all and sundry, that as much dared blink an eyelid.

It naturally followed, that "Not-So-Jolly-Porter" must suffer his cum-up-ance. Aware that their illustrious headmaster walked the Black Road from Phillack on Sunday mornings, two young Philp rebels, John and Steve, commandeered a row-boat, and with a plentiful supply of stones, rowed to Black Arch, and waited in ambush for their tormentor. The fusillade of missiles took Porter completely by surprise, and it was said, he sprinted the next fifty yards, in record time.

The following day, the swish of the cane, and the resultant howls from the miscreants, reverberated through the Wesleyan School.

Years later, after he had retired, the headmaster and my father recalled the incident. "Let's say", Porter smiled, "they were just high-spirited". That must have been the understatement of the year.

Feeding time at Mount Pleasant with seven hungry males at the table, was a bit hard on the girls. Generous helpings of bread were in constant demand, the girls stood at the head of the table, cutting the loaves furiously, in a vain attempt to keep pace with the seven famished appetites, whose ages ran from the very young, to the grown man.

The fact was, that with seven boys on the rampage, and their father away at sea, for most of the time, any semblance of parental control, was non-existent. As the boys reached adolescense and maturity, poaching was the occupying pastime. No 8 Mount Pleasant boasted a gun on every side of every beam in the kitchen, .22 rifles for the far target, 16 and 12 bore shotguns for the closer prey.

My father, being one of the very young offspring, fancied a single shot, bolt action .22, much lighter to handle than the heavier shotguns. With his mother absent for a few minutes, he climbed a chair and lifted the coveted messenger of destruction from its supporting nail. Snatching

Copperhouse Wesleyan School, (Senior Mixed). Headmaster: Thomas Jolly Porter. Ret'd 1920

Copperhouse Wesleyan School, (Senior Mixed). Circa 1919 (photo: M. Perry)

a few cartridges from a box on the sideboard, he retreated from the house to a far corner of the garden. After a few minutes, he lifted the gun to his shoulder and sighted the barrel on a large crow, perched on top of the clothes pole, oblivious to any impending danger.

Regretfully he had forgotten the family golden rule.

"Never, never, fire a gun within the confines of a garden". It was a good shot, the bullet passed through the crow, and the lifeless creature plummeted to the ground. The missile carried on down the garden, and with its high velocity, left only a small hole in the kitchen window. By this time mother Philp was back in the kitchen, engaged in ironing. She dropped the iron and screamed, as a noise like an express train whistled past her ear. There was a splintered crash, and her beautiful large framed print of the "Charge of the Light Brigade" suddenly disintegrated with glass flying everywhere.

A few minutes later, a small boy was nursing a very sore bottom, the rifle was returned to its rightful place on the beam, the baleful look in his mother's eye, did nothing to encourage further shooting adventures. His older brothers loudly declared, that he deserved a medal, for stopping the "Light Brigade" with only one bullet, but their mother was not amused.

The Captain's eldest son was Bob, an innervate reader of pulp fiction, but his scholastic ambitions extended no further, school was to be avoided at all cost. Invariably he played truant, so much so, that many notes were exchanged between his mother and Headmaster Porter, but all to no avail.

The Captain when ashore, seldom spent more than one night at home, then off to sea again, there was little time free, when working the "coasters". Away from his father's stern influence, Bob more or less went his own sweet way.

Eventually the truancy became so prevalent, that it reached the ears of the Captain. A wellwisher warned the erring son, that the "Sword of Damocles" was hovering overhead. Bob took the only way out. Whenever the "Ailsa" sailed into harbour, he disappeared completely, staying out all night, and sleeping rough, only returning home after the coaster had steamed over the bar, and headed once again into St Ives Bay.

Sadly Bob's well thought-out scheme went amiss, somehow or other, his calculations had fouled up.

He returned home after being out all night, to find his father firmly entrenched in the kitchen, with his feet soaking in the inevitable tub of hot water. There was no escape.

The Captain slowly wiped his feet dry, replaced his socks and slowly with deliberation, took a gun from the ceiling, and placed it on the table.

"Take off your shirt boy".

The young offender peeled off his vest and shirt.

"Put out your hands boy".

Bob knew what was coming, as he stretched out his hands, together, and with thumbs upwards. The Captain took some cord from a drawer of the kitchen sideboard, bound his sons thumbs together, then led him to the middle of the room. The loose end of the cord was thrown over the vacant nail on the ceiling beam, and pulled tight. Bob found himself lifted on to his toes, and awaited the impending punishment. William Henry unbuckled his belt, and gave his wayward offspring the thrashing of his life. The boy winced and squirmed under the merciless flogging, but refused to cry out, he knew his father would think less of him if he did. Finally released, he painfully sat on a chair, his whole body wracked with unbelievable agony. The Captain looked at him, and quietly said.

"From now on boy, you will go to school".

Bob didn't reply, but from then on he went to school, even Porter's ferocious discipline was preferable to his father's quiet wrath.

Although Bob's story may give the impression that William Henry was a hard, cruel, and unrelenting character, the seamen who worked with him, saw him in an entirely different light.

Our local ferryman, John (Jack) Couch knew him well, but I have often wondered how they fared together, the Captain never tolerated strong drink or profanity on board his ship. Jack, on the other hand, swore on practically every other word.

"You're a bl . . . . Philp", he said, looking me up and down.

"Naw that faice anywhere". Having affirmed my identity, he continued, "Sailed with your Great-granfer I did, on the 'Bessie Belle', bl . . . ole s . . . 'e was, we all 'ated his guts. William Henry was a different 'kettle-of fish', real gent, some of our locals sailed with him fer years".

It was true that "Tabby" Woolcock and "Robbie" Ellis worked on the "Ailsa" for such a long time, that the Captain regarded them as inseparable friends. When "Robbie" died, the then retired Captain, stood by the graveside and cried like a baby. "Manny" Ellis was another local that sailed on the "Ailsa" many times.

108

S.S. Ailsa
(photo: C. Stevens)

The cook prepared the meals for the Captain only, that was one of the privileges that went with the job. The crew provided their own food, anything that required re-heating, could be sent to the galley for a warm-up. Good cooks were not easy to come by, and there were occasions when the Captain took his wife along to attend to the galley, much to the approval of the crew, who often wangled an extra hot meal from the sympathetic lady.

Most of the coastal trips were of only a few days duration, leave ashore usually a few hours, or less, just long enough to stretch their sea-legs, get some food together, then back on board again.

During the school holidays, W.H. took one of his younger flock with him. My father accompanied him to Newport, Garston, and Cork, on a number of these excursions. Father was not a good sailor, at the first sign of a "Blow", he retreated to the cabin, where a kindly deck hand, gave him an old boot to spew into. If the "blow" turned to a gale, the reluctant young sailor was ordered to the bridge and wheelhouse, to

H.M.S. Montagu, aground at Lundy. 1906
(photo: unknown)

remain there until the storm had abated, under William Henry's eagle eye, mal-de-mer or not.

In May 1906, a dense fog enveloped the Bristol Channel, the Captain wisely decided to drop anchor off Lundy overnight, to await clearer weather. As far as my father was concerned, this was another night on the bridge, but with the sea motionless, there was, this time, no trouble with sea-sickness.

A ship hove-to in a fog, is a very errie experience, with visibility barely enough to see the deck, and of course, the claustrophobic silence that surrounds everything. Occasionally the faint sound of a fog-horn could be heard, but it was difficult to tell just what direction the sound came from. All night the Ailsa gently wallowed in the calm sea, sounding her fog-horn at frequent intervals.

"Well, what do you think of that?"

The lad raised himself from a fitful slumber, at the sound of "His Master's Voice". The fog had lifted with the early morning first light.

Less than a mile away, an unbelievable sight. A battle cruiser, had driven itself up, and on to the rocks.

H.M.S. Montagu was a 14,000 ton, first-class battle ship, commissioned only 3 years previously. Commanded by Capt' T.B.S. Adair, the great warship struck alongside the Shutter Rock, at 2- 10 AM, and there ignominiously ended its brief existence. For some unaccountable reason, the navigation must have been at variance, the first officers ashore, believed they were on the mainland. This afforded William Henry some amusement. Here was one of the Navy's latest fine battleships, with all the navigational refinements of the day, off course, and now suffering slow disintegration on the rocks of Lundy. Less than a mile away, the little Ailsa, safely at anchor, navigated through the fog to her position, with pin-point accuracy.

The cacophony of a 14,000 ton ship running itself on the rocks, can hardly be imaginable, but as my father pointed out, a landsman who had never experienced fog at sea, would never understand why the crew of the Ailsa had heard nothing.

Porpoise followed the coaster through the Bristol Channel, these large fish, up to 8 feet long, amused the lad with their antics. He watched them for miles, as they followed behind, plunging up and down in the sea.

The only sea monster he ever saw, was a giant Starfish, but with hindsight, it was probably a Sunfish. It appeared to be sunning itself just below the surface of the water, all 6 foot of it. Naturally anything that didn't conform to the norm', had to be caught and slaughtered. "Stop Engines" telegraphed from the wheelhouse, slowly the ship turned and drifted toward its intended victim. A deck-hand raced to the bow with a harpoon.

"When you're ready Fred", called the voice from the bridge. Fred threw the harpoon with unerring accuracy, striking the fish dead centre. There was a flurry in the water, and the fish with the harpoon firmly embedded, sank out of sight. The Captain almost flew off the bridge.

"Come on boys, all together, an' we'll drag 'er in".

Fred didn't move, "Sorry Cap", he wailed, "I forgot to tie up the line".

The loss of the fish and the harpoon, was too much to bear.

"Incompetent fools! Idiots!" for once in his life W.H. regretted his lack of fluency with sea-going profanity. Red-faced he retreated to the bridge, and spoke little to anyone for the rest of the day.

111

On another voyage, Bob's son Bill (on school holidays) was taken on board. A crew member on that trip, was the Captain's son Dick. It was only natural that Dick would keep an eye on the Captain's young grandson. Arriving at Cardiff they found it would be a few days to the next cargo. With little to do, Dick and Bill enjoyed themselves exploring the port, and the surrounding countryside. But all was not well back on the "Ailsa", the Captain was suffering an unwelcome distraction. Unfortunately the coaster had berthed just astern of a French Crabber. These small sailing vessels, had only the crudest of toilet facilities. To relieve himself, "Frenchie" squatted over a hole in the deck at the stern, the discarded waste dropping straight into the sea.

There had always been good-natured ribaldry between steam and sailing ships, but this time one of the French crew had decided to display an arrogance and contempt, which carried the joke beyond the pale.

When in harbour, on a sunny morning, the Captain liked to breakfast on the bridge, and each morning Dick carried the tray from the galley, to his father firmly seated in his favourite chair, but one morning W.H. seemed uneasy.

"Don't go Dick, I want to show you something, just watch the 'Frenchie'".

Dick watched, one of the French crew had come to the stern of the crabber, and pulled down his trousers. Instead of using the deck hole, he sat on the stern rail, with his back to the Captain, and proceeded to do what nature required.

"He's done that every morning we've been tied up here, and always just when I'm about to have my breakfast, you know boy, that's carrying things a bit too far".

Dick thought the whole business hilarious, but he could see that his father had taken it rather badly, and decided to resolve the situation.

"Leave it to me dad, I'll guarantee there will be no repeat performance after tomorrow".

Later that morning, Dick and Bill walked from the quay and into town. The market was in full swing, and Dick soon found what he was looking for, a butcher's stall. He had a few words with the proprietor. Into an empty tobacco tin, the butcher ladled some thick animal's blood. "So far, so good", grinned Dick, "now for a Corn Chandler". Bill looked on, a little puzzled, but knowing that all would be revealed in good time. At the corn shop, a handful of wheat disappeared into an envelope. "Now", Dick winked, "back to the ship and prepare our little surprise for 'Johnny Frenchman'".

Back on the Ailsa, Dick turned to Bill, "Get the ole 16 bore boy", A few minutes later Bill placed the shotgun on the table.

The old single barrel hammer gun had seen better days. The stock was full of shakes, and the barrel pitted. No one could recall how it came to be on the Ailsa, it had always seemed to have been there. At times one of the crew would resurrect the ancient fire- arm, and blaze away at some unsuspecting creature, in the distance.

Dick took one of the cartridges, and with a penknife carefully rolled back the front edge, lifted out the card disc, and with a clatter, emptied the cartridge of its lead shot.

The tobacco tin of animals' blood was now produced, the cover taken off, the wheat added, and the mess stirred to a thick pastelike consistency. Into the cartridge case Dick spooned the revolting concoction, and replaced the card disc.

"That should do the trick very nicely", he murmured, as he peened over the outer edge of the cartridge with his thumb nail.

It was Bill that took the Captain's breakfast to the bridge, the next morning. William Henry asked no questions, he had seen Dick lurking about on the deck, finally finding himself a comfortable position behind the for'ard hatch. Something was about to happen, he deemed it prudent to know little about it.

Right on cue Frenchie made his appearance, bared his posterior, sat on the sternrail, and proceeded to display natures natural functions. There was a flash from behind the hatch, followed by a loud bang. With a howl of dismay, Frenchie jumped into the air, clutched at his bottom, then the horror of it all, he brought his hands away covered in, what seemed to be, human flesh and blood. Panic stricken he ran up the deck, screaming like a Banshee.

What he and his shipmates thought about it, when they discovered that his fatal wounding was nothing more than a number of little bruises over his bare skin, we shall never know, suffice that the next morning, the Captain breakfasted without incident. Later that day, the Ailsa took on cargo, steamed out of Cardiff, out into the Bristol Channel, and home.

It was a sad day for William Henry when he walked down the gangplank of the Ailsa for the last time. The old coaster had weathered its last storm, battered and worn out, she was designated for the scrap-yard.

113

A few weeks later he was offered another command, a much larger vessel, the S.S. Poultney. She had been for sale for some time, on the mud flats of the Tyne. With a heavy heart, and a few stalwarts from the Ailsa, he journeyed by train, to Newcastle.

The ship was afloat each day at high tide, and appeared to be in fairly good condition. Three days later, with the necessary documents signed, and a quantity of coal taken on board, they steamed down the Tyne, and out into the North Sea.

With a strong gale blowing (Beaufort Scale 9, wind vel' 44 mph) the sea was very choppy, but there was something more serious, a problem the Captain had not envisaged.

The larger ship was plunging into the on-coming waves, and then sluggishly struggling to the surface. Each time this happened there was little answer at the helm, for those few moments, the Poultney was virtually without a rudder.

The Captain remembered the time, when a huge wave caught the Ailsa, bow-on, completely covering the little ship with a wall of water. She gallantly popped up to the surface, shook herself like a duck, then sailed on, as if nothing had happened. He prayed that no such wave would ever engulf the Poultney, he could visualise the headlines, "Lost at sea without trace".

And so began a very uneasy relationship between the Captain and the Poultney. Unknown to anyone, including himself, William Henry was on the verge of a nervous breakdown. The final blow came while in Port at Garston, Liverpool. He left the ship for a stroll through the streets, and out into the country, by the late evening he had not returned.

The crew turned out to search for him, they knew his favourite haunts, and eventually found him sitting near the edge of a wood, his head in his hands. The local doctor diagnosed, acute nervous exhaustion, with a lifetime at sea and now past his prime, his health had taken its toll. A temporary skipper was appointed to bring the vessel back to Hayle, and my grandfather returned via train.

Some weeks later, refreshed by his enforced break, William Henry packed his suitcase, and in a not-too-happy state of mind, walked from his home at Mount Pleasant to North Quay, to take command once again. The temporary skipper was waiting at the end of the gang-plank.

"I saw you coming, and came to meet you".

W.H. looked at the young man, he knew what was coming next.

"You know of course", continued the skipper, "that I shall probably never get another opportunity of being in command, by coming back you have ruined everything I'd hoped for, taken away my job and my future".

William Henry fixed the distraught seaman with a balisick stare.

"I don't want your job sonny, and as far as 'that' is concerned", he pointed to the Poultney, "you can stick it right up your backside".

With as much dignity as he could muster, he picked up his suitcase and walked from the quay. He hated swearing, that must have been the nearest he ever came to it.

William Henry never again walked down to the harbour, and never looked at another ship, when he talked about his seafaring days, he only mentioned his beloved "Ailsa".

During the "Great War", he worked for a time at the Dynamite Works, but ill health finally drove him into early retirement.

At times my father called to see him, usually on a Sunday morning, and it was on one of these visits that I was taken along. It was the first and last time I saw the Captain, that I remember.

The end came quite suddenly. The Captain had been talking to my father, about the "old days" and of course the "Ailsa", which had been so much a part of him. He paused in mid sentence,

"Leonard, will you fill my pipe for me, a quiet smoke might do me good?"

Father took the briar from the table, walked across to the mantelpiece, and filled the pipe from the tobacco jar, turned again to the table, but the old man hadn't moved.

Eliza came into the room and looked at her husband,

"Is it?" – "Is he?" –

"It's all over mother, just as he would have wanted".

With the "Ailsa" safely tied up at North Quay, Captain William Henry Philp had telegraphed from the bridge for the last time.

"Finish with engines".

Twilight and evening bell,
And after that the dark!
And may there be no sadness of farewell
When I embark.

A. Tennyson (Wr & Pub 1889)

115

*Copperhouse Wesleyan School. Infants No. 2. Mistress: Miss Julia Ann Newton,
(early 1900's)
Photo: F. Thomas)*

*Copperhouse Wesleyan School. Infants (early 1900's)
Mistress: J. A. Newton (right)
(photo: F. Thomas)*

116

Bodriggy Street. Circa 1905
(photo: L. Hosken)

Lifeboat Day. Foundry Square. Hayle. Circa 1909. Lifeboat: Admiral Rodd
(photo: C. Smith)

117

Loading 'Sugarbeet' at Hayle. (date unknown)
Note: Potato Forks

'Celebrity' – grounded on Hayle Bar. Circa 1968
(photo: R. Williams)

20

Clouds and darkness are around him –
Psalm 97:2

"He was like a Greek God", that was how my Aunt Elsie described him. His other brothers and sisters also referred to him in glowing terms, tall, a fine physique, and exceptionally good looking. I have to take their word for it, because Uncle Stephen (Stee) died in America when I was only 2 years old. However, over the years, the family spoke about him so often, that I feel I know him, very well indeed. Regardless of all his shortcomings, or perhaps because of them, Stee seemed to have been, the family's favourite son.

He was an excellent shot with a .22 rifle, and often represented the town "Volunteers" at the small bore competitions. His target work was so good that some of the competitors objected to him using his own rifle for these advents, and for a time Stee had to make-do with a government issue weapon. He was equally good with a double-barrel shot-gun, and would show off his expertise, by shooting two rabbits on the run, reloading, then bag the third, before it reached the sanctuary of its burrow. For some unknown reason, his shooting was very erratic above the sky- line, wild duck and wood pidgeons went safely on their way, after he had pulled the triggers.

So much for the sportsman, for there was a darker side to his personality – Stee was an alcoholic –

During periods of obsessive drinking, the mantle of the happy-go-lucky fellow dropped away, revealing another, altogether different side to his character.

On a drinking spree in the "Cornish Arms", Stee became tacturn and withdrawn, the constant teasing by a little agitator (five foot four in his socks) had found its mark. With a squeal of fear, the agitator suddenly found himself suspended in mid-air, his neck held by two hands, in a vice-like grip. It took three men to pull them apart, the object of his

119

attack slumping to the floor, hardly knowing whether he was in this world or the next.

The outcome of this fracas, was that Stee appeared in court, found guilty of malicious intent and assault, and fined £2 (quite a lot of money in those days). He had little money himself, so, as always, his mother stepped in and settled the account.

The drink had such a hold, that he would go missing for days at a time, only to be found sleeping it off under a hedge-row. His cronies would borrow a builder's handcart, or if that was not readily available, a wheelbarrow, and Stee would be trundled back to Mount Pleasant in this undignified manner, accompanied by the grins of his numerous helpers, who provided the motive force of the conveyance. Finally implanting him in the comparative safety of his bed, and under the eagle eye of his mother.

In the throes of "delirium tremens", Stee would lie on his back in sweat and terror. Large black spiders crawled over the walls, horrid little creatures from another world, stared and obscenely grimaced at him from the bottom of the bed. These horrors lasted about four days, then came the remorse and depression. Crying like a baby, he promised his mother that he would never drink again. But Stee's good resolutions were doomed to failure, and it wouldn't be long before the booze once again, took the upper hand. It was during one of these alcoholic binges, that something very strange and incomprehensible happened.

Stee had been missing for some days, and then, approaching midnight, he suddenly burst through the front door. For a few moments he stood behind the closed door, trying hard to get some kind of co-ordination from his befuddled brain, bloodshot eyes stared blankly at his mother.

She looked at her son in despair, he was unshaven, his clothes torn and splattered with mud, obviously he had slept wherever he had fallen down. But there was something else, deep in those demented eyes, she saw lurking, an unbelievable terror.

"What's happened son? what have you seen?" Stee looked wildly about him.

"They're after me mother, the angels of hell are after me". He snatched the old cutlass from the wall, and stumbled up the stairs, reached the landing, and sat on the old seaman's trunk. From this vantage point, he had a clear view of the descending staircase, and the front door.

With the cutlass nestling across his lap, he prepared himself for battle with the unknown.

Suddenly there was a noise like a rumble of thunder, the front door shook, almost bursting from its hinges, the whole house trembled as if in the grip of an earth tremor. For about a minute the terror continued, and then, just as suddenly as it started, it stopped.

It was some time later, that his mother finally summoned up enough courage to cautiously open the door, and peer into the street. All was quiet, just a normal frosty, clear, winter's night, not a soul to be seen, the rest of the street asleep behind lightless windows.

What really happened that night?

The obvious explanation is, that his drinking companions followed him home, and scared the living daylights out of him. To be chased by the sound of clanking chains and supernatural howls, would have been a terrifying experience, to the stoutest of hearts, let alone one already in the throes of DTs. The final assault on the house itself, must have reduced Stee and his mother to frightened wrecks.

The odd thing about it, was the next day. His mother told the neighbours about their scary experience, but the neighbours had heard nothing. She was a very old lady indeed when I asked her about it.

"I suppose", she said, "it must have been a prank, his drinking companions were a pretty rough set, but when I recall that awful look in his eyes, I sometimes wonder, did he really see, the Angels of Hell?"

Not long after, Stee became a reformed character, but it took more than a visitation from the fiends of the Nether World, to turn him from the booze. Simply, Stee had fallen in love.

Mary Pascoe was a beautiful girl, they courted for nearly two years, under Mary's calming influence, he rid himself of the curse of alcoholism. But Stee had been unemployed for a long time, and reformed drunks were considered unemployable.

In desperation he realised there was only one option open. Go to his three brothers in America, work with them in the mines, and save enough money to enable Mary to join him at some later date. Together they would start a new life, in a new world.

And so the die was cast, Stee borrowed the passage money from his mother, promising to pay it back, as soon as he commenced working. (In those days, steerage passengers could travel to the USA for £12 or less).

At Hayle railway station, Mary kissed him goodbye, and gave him a gold ring. "Keep this my love, in remembrance of me".

"I'll never part with it", he whispered, "but I'll soon be sending for you, then all our troubles will be behind us".

They waved to each other until the train steamed out of the station. Through her tears she watched the coaches, until they rounded the bend and disappeared under the bridge. Now out of sight all she could hear was the fading sound of the locomotive.

"Oh Stee", she sobbed, "I'll never see you again, not in this world".

A few weeks later, Stee joined his brothers, John, Dick, and Will, in Butte City, Montana, and was soon working with them at the "Anaconda" copper mine. He wrote to Mary, extolling the virtues of that wonderful country, promising to send for her, as soon as he had saved enough money.

But away from Mary's steadying influence, Stee soon drifted back into his old ways. He lost his job, and became the town drunk, laughed at and despised by all.

At first he had lodged at his brother's John's house, but then he moved out, and eventually ended up in a doss-house, on the edge of town, with, what Dick referred to, "The scum of the territory". By this time he was so ashamed of himself that he avoided his brothers, as much as possible. Letters to his mother and Mary, had now stopped altogether.

It was my Uncle Will who filled in part of the story. "I was saddened to see my brother, that I remembered as such a fine, good looking man, now reduced to a shambling wreck, with his clothes in tatters, begging for a hand-out from some kind passer- by. I realised he could never survive a winter in Butte, without some help. I went along to the cobblers, (working boots were hand-made in the mining towns). 'For God's sake "Jo", make him a pair of good boots to see him through the winter'. I gave him the size and paid the bill. 'Jo' promised he would make them immediately, and at the first opportunity tell Stee to come to the shop and collect. A few weeks later I was passing the shop, when 'Jo' called me inside.

"I've seen him Will, told him about the boots, but he hasn't been near the place. Look here boy, he's not interested in boots, buy him a bottle of Rye, he'll go away into some corner, and be happy for a little while".

I pocketed the money, snow was already falling, and my brother was somewhere out there, ill equipped for the winter, but where?"

The three brothers were very concerned, winters in the Rocky Mountains can hardly be called pleasant, with blizzards common- place, the on-coming season was no exception.

There had been no news of Stee for some time. Three very worried

122

Dick, Will and John. Butte City, Montana
(photo: C. Stevens)

Richard Philp (Uncle Dick)
(photo: R. Davey)

brothers decided it was time to round-up the stray, by force if necessary, and get him lodged at a decent near-by place, where they could keep a wary eye on him. Night after night, the three trudged the snow-bound streets, hunted the barns and saloon back rooms, but to no avail. At the doss-house they were met by sullen stares. "Haven't seen him, must be sleeping it off somewhere". Outside Dick paused for a moment, "That scum are lying", he said, "they know where he is".

After nights of fruitless search, they had to admit defeat, Stee had vanished from the face of the earth.

In the following spring, two young lads on an exploration trip, in the foothills of the Rockies, happened on an old line-shack, the kind that cowboys sometimes use as an over-night resting place. They pushed open the door and peered into the small windowless room. The light from the doorway spilled over the floorboards. In the far corner was, what appeared to be, a sack or a bundle. Closer inspection revealed a human corpse. It was in a seated position, with the head dropped to his folded arms. Alongside was an empty bottle.

Later that day, two exhausted lads were reporting their find to the Sheriff of Butte. A horse and waggon was quickly hitched, then the Sheriff, with a deputy and the two lads, rode out to the line-shack, to retrieve the body.

That afternoon, John, Dick, and Will, were called out of the mine and told to report to the mortuary immediately.

The Sheriff met them at the gate, "I'm afraid it's Stee", he said, "he's been dead a long time, what's left of him is unrecognisable, still, as his brothers, you might be able to make a positive identification".

Dick picks up the story;

"I knew it was Stee as soon as I entered that place, even before I saw the body. He was lying on a stone slab. Rats and other small animals had eaten away the face, and parts of his body. The corpse was in such a state of putrification it was obvious he had been dead for some months. There was no positive way to identify the body, then I noticed Mary's gold ring, still on the third finger of his left hand. The three of us agreed, that this was our brother".

When the inquest was held, the verdict was a foregone conclusion. It was simply, that Stephen Philp, for some unknown reason, was tramping in the mountains. When a storm threatened he sought refuge in the line-shack. Trapped by the blizzard's fury, and with no hope of getting back to town, he sat huddled on the floor, drank the bottle of whisky, and folded his hands under his armpits, for a little warmth, and waited.

After a time his head lolled forward to his chest, he drifted into a deep sleep – and – slowly froze to death –

"Dick never accepted the verdict.

"What was my brother doing, tramping in the mountains, in the depths of winter, without even a decent overcoat?" He lit his pipe, "Were they trying to tell us, that he walked all that way just to find a cabin and drink a bottle of whisky. In that weather, no way, he would have found a hide-a-way somewhere in town, he'd done it many times before. My brother lived with the scum of the earth, they'd cut your throat for a dollar". He paused, looked at me, then continued, "Dessie boy, they poisoned him, put his body on a cart, and took him to that cabin. An empty bottle alongside, would make it look as if he had drunk himself to death, the on-coming blizzard covered the tracks perfectly".

Dick peered at me over the blackened bowl of his pipe, his eyes mist with emotion.

"I know he was poisoned Dessie, and I know the b . . . who did it".

I asked Uncle Will for his version of the tragedy.

"Dick", he said, "was very emotional, and claimed that Stee was poisoned, and over the years nothing would shake that belief. The thought of Stee being murdered, was a little too bizarre for me, and I accepted the verdict of the inquest. However, since those days, I've gone over, in my mind countless times, the evidence as it was presented, and also the veiled hints and rumours circulating around Butte at that time. In retrospect, I must now admit, that I believe Dick was right".

The truth of the tragedy we shall never know for certain. My own conclusions, gleaned from members of the family, can only be conjecture – Here it is for what it's worth –

Stee was a handy man with his fists, and we know that the other inmates of the doss-house, were no match for him. At times, when suffering from DTs, he would smash the furniture and severely beat up, any that stood in his way, before lapsing into a stupor. It was, I believe, during one of these quieter moments, while Stee was still sleeping-it-off, that they loaded him on to a cart, and took him into the mountains, callously left to die of exposure. An empty bottle alongside completed the picture. By the time he came-to, and with a storm approaching, any chance of getting back to Butte, was out of the question. The fact that it was many months before he was discovered, was an added bonus to the cover-up.

But then – who knows – ?

After my grandfather died, my grandmother added her son's name to the tombstone.

Just to the left-hand side of the path, in the old cemetery at Phillac you can still see his memorial:

"Also Stephen His Son Died in USA 1926 Aged 45".

> They buried him deep; 'neath the old willow tree,
> The mourners that day; numbered but three,
> Carved on a wood cross; in letters entwined,
> "Our brother – our friend – who ran out of time".
> From; "Song of Tragedy" by Des Philp, 1990.

21

The "Moloch"

"It's nothing but a dirty d . . . thing". My mother eyed the kitchen range (Slab) with revulsion. The "thing" glared back at her in defiance. All houses boasted a Slab, but mother looked on it as symbol of working class slavery.

Only when the top-plate glowed to a dull red, was it ready for cooking or baking. It devoured buckets of coal to a gluttonous degree, the coal sold as "Best" was suitable, but the cheaper "Nut" coal seemed to create more dust than heat.

Some of the Slabs in our street, would delight a museum today, with the iron-work daily blackened and the brass knobs gleaming with liberal applications of "Brasso". But not so in our house, a rub with a black-lead brush, once a week. The brassware suffering the indignity of a quick burnish with a fine, but well worn, piece of emery cloth.

Our "Moloch" provided the means of cooking, drying the herbs and damp clothes, was a constant source of hot water, for washing and drinking, not forgetting the weekly bath.

Pilchards steeped in vinegar and spiced with Bay leaves, plundered from a hedge at Phillack Rectory, slowly simmered all afternoon. Of all the pleasantries of those far-off days, the lingering, mouth-watering smell of marinated pilchards, still remain the most unforgettable of my culinary memories.

Pilchards could often be purchased at a penny each, from two brothers of St Ives origin. A ferocious pair, forever arguing, and often settling the score with a punch-up, they drove their horse-and-cart from street to street, bawling,

"Pi-ards fresh Pi-ards".

The hectoring pair stood in the cart, knee deep in fish, levelling curses at the housewives, who insisted on getting the best value for their penny.

Caroline Carthew with her niece Hazel Teuling, recall old memories under the watchful eye of the Cornish Slab. Circa 1961
(photo: R. Williams)

My mother hated buying from them, but the fish, caught just the night before, was of prime quality. She picked up her selection, paid the money, and without saying a word, walked back to the house, pretending not to hear the string of profanity hurled at her.

By the time the cart had wound its way from the street to the edge of town, and to the more affluent, the price of fish had doubled. This fact did not escape the eagle eye of those, "To the Manor born", they had their own way of dealing with felonous interlopers. One of their "domestics" was sent into the street, with orders to purchase at the basic

128

rate. Forgetting to reimburse her when she returned, was an added economical advantage.

All the affluent were dedicated Christians, and attended a place of worship with devotional regularity. But then, so they should, they had so much to be thankful for.

"Though I speak with the tongues of men
and of angels, and have not charity,
I am become as sounding brass, or a
tinkling cymbal".

1 Corinthians 13:1

As a young lad, pasty-making fascinated me. First the pastry was rolled out thinly, a deft curl of the knife (utilising a dinner plate as a template) reduced it to eight or more inches diameter. On one half, thinly slices potatoes were heaped, with some turnip, and a little onion, topped with chopped beef. If the beef was lean, a dab of butter assisted the baking. A sprinkle of pepper and salt, and, if desired, a sprig of parsley for flavouring. The other half of the pasty was then turned over, and the edges swiftly crimped together with skilled fingers.

Cornish pasties were NEVER made from minced beef and diced potatoes. The ingredients were always introduced RAW, and cooked inside the pastry.

Leslie Banks, the film actor, enjoyed a pasty. Arriving on holiday, his first "port-of-call" was Iris Angove's cottage.

"Please, Mrs Angove make me one of your delicious pasties". The lady could hardly refuse, and Leslie sat in the small kitchen, and watched, until the Slab finally came up trumps.

"Matthew, Mark, Luke and John,
Ate a pasty, five foot long,
Bit it once; and bit it twice,
Oh my gosh; it's full of mice".

In the depths of winter, we found another use for our Slab. The "Shiver" (oven shelf) made an excellent bed-warming-pan.

Cleaning the innards of a Cornish Slab, was a messy problem. Once a year father pilgrimaged to the garden, carrying the oven casing, covered in soot. After a thorough clean with a stiff brush, he returned it to its rightful place.

Chimney sweeping was a much more simple, but perilous operation. He climbed over the rooftop, and dropped a weighted Furze bush (tied to a cord) down the chimney. Prospective sweeps looking for business in our street, suffered a very lean time indeed.

My mother had a love-hate relationship with the "Moloch", modern day equivalents failed to impress.

The Slab remained in her kitchen, until the day she died.

22

One day at a time

"Churky Pile" was the name we gave to an in-fill alongside the old Copperhouse Canal. Waste ash from the Electric Works had, over many years, filled and levelled out a large area. When I was a young lad, residue ash was still being added to a pile at one end, alongside "Allen's" garage.

In the early morning's light, gangs of boys armed with buckets and sacks, waited impatiently for the dumping lorries.

After they had arrived and tipped their loads, the gangs furiously scrabbled all over the pile, searching for pieces of coke, the size of a small walnut. They returned to the street with their pitiful collection, and at times, with nothing at all.

With the modernisation of the coal firing plant, at the Power Station, and the residue now reduced to black sand, dumping at "Churky Pile" ceased.

The name still persisted, It was here the boys stacked their "May Day" and "Guy Fawke's" bonfires.

Furze bushes were ravished from the mine burrows at Wheal Alfred, over a mile away, and huge piles, locked by a strong rope, were dragged and coaxed by many young and willing hands, along the roads, to the "Pile". Many foraging trips would ensure a "fire" at least twelve foot high.

Furze burns very easily, even in wet weather, and with the addition of household rubbish, and a nest of rubber tyres from Allen's garage, underneath, success was assured.

Security was another matter, the "Fire" was quite a way from the street, and it wasn't possible to mount a twenty-four hour guard.

On one occasion a teenage misfit set it alight, burning most of it to the ground. Unfortunately for him, he was spotted leaving the scene of his arson.

The lads chased him all the way to his home, pelting him with wet tobs and stones. After the avenging horde had departed, the mother tearfully reported the assault of her precious off-spring, to the Police Station. Sergeant Turner looked at her and exploded.

"Serves him b . . . well right".

Ventonleague had the largest of all Hayle bonfires. George Ingram, a local farmer, pulled masses of Furze, with a horse and cart. The resulting stack was so high, that the men of the village took charge, using ladders to reach the top.

Ventonleague still celebrate with a huge bonfire, but only once a year, on November 5th.

Kites were a favourite pastime of the older boys. Box kites, square and triangular kites, sporting tails as long as ten feet, (made from rolled newspaper and string). Kite fights were popular, and the red, white and blue circles, courageously battled with the black crosses. Within a very short time, hours of patience, care and loving toil, would lie shattered in the grass.

Regattas at Ventonleague pond, were also the in-thing. Ingeniously carved model boats, with chicken feathers mounted across a strip of timber near the stern, enabled the wind to whisk them along, at a remarkable turn of speed. A piece of tin stuck into the stern, could be bent, to give the model a better sense of direction. Only boats that sailed the full length of the pond, without stopping, qualified for championship status.

In those days, children created their own pastimes, kites and feather boats cost nothing to make. Younger children did not associate with the older breed, so we stood back and watched the fun.

Fully mustered, our gang numbered just five. Jack Harris, John Kneebone, Billy Woolcock, Barrie Allen and myself, but often we split up, in twos or threes.

During the winter evenings, our outdoor games were of the utmost simplicity.

"Jack, Jack, Show-Light", the keeper of the candle lantern, hunts down the hidden-a-way prey, then race him back to the starting point. "Urky", was similar, but played without a lantern, first one back to the post, shouted, "One, Two, Three, Urky".

Fed up with "Show Light" and "Urky", we could always amuse ourselves by tying a few doors together, and watch our superior grown-ups struggling to open them. Many doors still had latches, ideal for delinquents, bent on evil intent. The Bodriggy Street Boys invented a novel twist to the door tying.

132

Instead of immediately running away, they stayed by the two doors, and watched the fun. First one door and then the other would be tugged, accompanied by the vilest of curses, and threatened retribution. After a time the inevitable happened, the cord stretched, just enough to allow the door to open, and a hand to squeeze through, a hand bearing a sharp implement, namely a knife. Still the BSB stood their ground, it was now time for the coup de grace. One of the gang produced a bunch of freshly cut stinging nettles, which he generously daubed on the knife hand. The howls of torment could be heard the length of the street. It was now time to beat a hasty retreat, they knew full well, that the next time they saw that hand, it would be suitably protected by a towel or a glove.

Jack (Jimmie) Clemence, was a boot-tapper (cobbler) and conducted his business from a tumble-down hut in the garden, at nearby Cross Street. He often worked late into the night, his sole illumination in that domain, was, one-candle-power. It was a simple matter to negotiate the side path access, quietly open the hut door, blow out the candle, jam the door shut, and then retreat to a safe distance.

With all the junk in that hut, how he managed to finally extract himself, without breaking a leg, was a mystery never solved. Muttering devilish incantations, he returned to the house, to fetch the solitary box of matches. One box per household, was norm' in those days.

The long summer days are best remembered. "Yo-Yo" and "Tops" enjoyed brief moments of glory, not forgetting the inevitable "Marbles" with names like, "Chalkies", "Alleys", "Popshies" (salvaged from "Pop" bottles) and the very large "Town Dribblers".

There was of course, the old standby "Kit".

"Kit" was a piece of wood approx' four inches long, sharpened to a point, at each end. A sharp rap on the point, with a short stick, and the "Kit" would fly upwards, to be struck again, and land some yards away. The striker shouts, "I'll give you 'X' paces". Failure by the opposition, to make back to the "Off" spot, by that number (usually unattainable) would be added to the striker's score.

Our cricket equipment was of the very best. If a bat wasn't readily obtainable, the situation was easily solved by roughly cutting one from a piece of scrap wood. Stumps were represented by two stones, the preferred wooden ball was illicitly obtained from under the rear canvas of "Anderton & Rowlands" coco-nut shy.

We often contented ourselves with a tut-a-round in the old school yard, now reduced to a flat square level, devoid of fence or wall, and level with the street. The nearby residents lived in a state of hypertension, knowing full well that their windows beckoned disintegration.

Jack Harris and myself were indulging in the noble game of cricket, when suddenly the wooden ball sliced to one side, and one of Leonard Morris's window panes, was no more. We didn't run away, there was no point, he knew us too well, we just stood our ground, dumbstruck, and awaited our deserved dressing down.

The door opened, Leonard emerged into the sunlight, inspected the damage, then turned to us with a quiet voice.

"You broke it – You repair it".

He knew this was an impossible task for two young boys, but didn't see it that way. It was a challenge, and we accepted it.

I found some putty in father's workshop, and Jack located two discarded picture frames, with the glass intact. Alas we had no glass cutter, but we remembered an odd story. Someone in the distant past had mentioned, that glass could be cut under water – with a scissors – There was nothing to lose, and a little later, in Jack's back kitchen, two young lads could be seen, bent over a bath tub, their hands deep in water.

It actually worked, but in our excitement we cracked the first pane. With a little more care and patience, the second emerged from the watery depths triumphantly cut to size. The bruising and soreness of our hands, tenderized even more so by the water, seemed a small price to pay for ultimate success.

The job finally accomplished, we asked the resident to inspect the repair. Leonard Morris looked at the window pane in bewilderment.

"How on earth", he asked, "did you manage to cut the glass?" Jack assumed an air of unsmiling feigned innocence.

"With a scissors, Mr Morris".

Leonard paused, looked at us, then roared with laughter. He was still laughing when he re-entered the house and closed the door. I looked at Jack and said, "I have this feeling that he didn't believe us".

Uncle Dick popped in at No 22, and put his latest prize find on the kitchen table.

"I looked over the causeway wall, and there it was, on the top of a pile of rubbish", he enthused.

Father picked up the Walking-Stick-Gun with curiosity. Dick had obviously spent some time cleaning the weapon, the moving parts were now nicely oiled and smoothly working, but the wooden handle was no longer in evidence.

"You're the carpenter of the family", said Dick, with a glint in his eye. Without further ado, father found himself conscripted into making the necessary wooden handle.

That weekend, the three Philps, Dick, Bill, and my father, sauntered down to the "Mud" for the sole purpose of putting their new-found toy through its paces. Dick, being the proud owner, naturally elected himself as "first shot". Sitting on a public bench, he slewed around to use the seat back as a firing rest. Pushing one of his home-made, extra-power cartridges, into the breach, he sighted the barrel on a wild duck, just within range, and gently squeezed the trigger.

There was a deafening roar. Father described the scene as the most hilarious, he had ever witnessed. The gun barrel split and blew apart, Dick was left with something that resembled a smoking, peeled banana. He glared from under his scorched eyebrows, hardly knowing what had happened.

"Bloody thing", he raved, and threw the shattered weapon, far out into the water.

Father and Bill often retold the story, amid fits of laughter, but for some unknown reason, Dick never seemed to appreciate the joke.

At times, on a Sunday, my parents attended a place of evening worship, and reluctantly I had to tag along. Churches were seldom visited, and Chapels were not considered. They expected a "Silver" collection, that meant sixpence or more, anyone with the gall to contribute a thrup-penny silver piece, for all to see, on the wooden collection plate, was silently excommunicated on the spot. So there was only one place to give thanks to the Lord, the "Salvation Army", where even a penny was gratefully received. My parents held no deep religious conviction, a visit to the "Army", compensated to some extent, for a very dull day.

The upper floor of the old slag-built warehouse, on the edge of Copperhouse Dock and alongside "Daniel's" grocery and clothing emporium (formerly Bazeley's), was sadly, the "Citadel", although no-one ever referred to it by such an exhalted name. It was simply the "Hall", the irreverent pronounced it "ole".

To gain entrance, we first negotiated the outside, slippery, wooden steps, then through the door, and into the "Hall" itself.

It was an appalling place. The floor repaired in many places, with pieces of flattened tin, nailed over the offending gaps. Light from the gas and oil lamps, barely reflected from the whitewashed walls and ancient bare roof trusses. The rostrum at the far end, was illuminated a little better, after all, it was here the action would take place.

Every Sunday the "Hall" was packed, with services of two hours or more. Some of the really dedicated, worked themselves into a religious fervour, and the singing of, "When the roll is called up yonder", rocked the rafters. Tommy Drew accompanied the five- piece brass band, on the bass drum, and then would suddenly stand up and deliver his testimony, which lasted equally as long as the Captain's sermon. No-one ever went to sleep at that gathering, in any case, the hard, torturous, forms we sat on, saw to that. Even the rats, that infested the building, came out of hiding, to join in with the rejoicing, I watched fascinated, as they ran across the roof truss tie, just above the head of the preacher.

In the mid' 1930s, Adjutant Garner and his wife, were directed to Hayle and given the dubious honour of "Guardians of the flock". He immediately set to work, reorganising, an act of faith that was not always appreciated.

The first priority was a decent place for people to worship in. A piece of ground was purchased at Cross Street, and then the adjutant took a big gamble. He persuaded the Army committee to take the plunge, and put into motion, the building of a new "Hall".

Adjutant, Mrs Garner and Wesley. 1936

On Jan' 9th 1936, the foundation stones were laid by our local notables. It took many years to pay off the mortgage, but today the Salvation Army have a decent place to worship in.

Still – I was sorry to see the old building demoted to a store, and years later demolished.

The Witchcraft and Fraudulent Mediums Act of 1735, wasn't repealed until 1951. The police, with little else to do, kept an eye open for fortune tellers and similarly dubious characters, but their vigilance proved fruitless. Even reading the tea-cups, was considered a dicey business, those who indulged were looked on as emissaries of the Devil. Small groups of women, congregated behind locked doors, and stirred the witches brew.

A lady from Bodriggy Street was the contact, she seemed to have a flair with the leaves. After many cups of tea, and with all her subjects happy at the thought of a fortune in the offing, she picked up the collection, and departed. At least the tea-leaves had been kind to her.

My mother was also a dab-hand at the leaves. When she was employed at the Dynamite Works, the mid-day break was often punctuated by a session into the occult, but she admitted to me, that it was just a load of rubbish.

Uncle Will made one of his rare appearances, we didn't see him all that often, as he lived two miles away at Chenhalls, near St Erth.

His old Cornish Slab had wheezed its last, and Will had purchased another, admittedly second-hand but in a much better condition. Removing the redundant Slab, he found another little stove, built into the side of the hearth, a relic from the past, and obviously from the days prior to the Slab design. Behind the stove, lo' and behold! a Witch Bottle. These bottles came in various sizes, often utilizing an old earthenware pot for the purpose. But this one was exceptional. Made of iron, a little larger than a cricket ball, hollow, but with a small hole. Through the hole, a number of pins would be inserted, followed by a liberal supply of urine. Built into the wall, just behind the stove, it afforded everlasting protection against the "Evil Eye". If the hole became blocked, and the heat from the stove incurred a minor explosion, what better proof that the Witch Bottle was doing its stuff.

When I removed a fireplace at Bodriggy Street, in 1956, I was amazed to find one of these little stoves, still in the side of the chimney hearth. Not facing, but end on to the kitchen. I remembered Uncle Will, and his "find", and I looked for a "Witch Bottle", but I looked in vain.

137

Some houses boasted a wind-up gramophone, ours was a "Columbia", a rather nice machine, with the sound outlet, built in. I don't know where it came from, probably someone gave it to us. They must have given us the records also, because we never bought any.

I was forbidden to play the "Classics", on ten or twelve inch discs, the dulcet tones of Dame Clara Butt, were not for my grubby ears. I contented myself with the six and seven inch records, that our benefactor had purchased from Woolworth's, with trade names like "Broadcast" and "Eclipse".

I can still hear those tunes, "I want to be alone with Mary Brown", "Betty Co-ed", "Stein Song", and the inevitable "Ridgeway Parade", a kind of a potted concert, on one small disc.

The Kneebones sported a gramophone with a large metal horn. This gave a much louder and brasher sound than our "Columbia". On this I heard, Cole Porter's "Miss Otis Regrets", and a war recording, which intrigued me, General —— farewell to his troops'. (Surely a collector's gem today).

By the mid' 1930s, the Wireless was the desired thing.

Willie Andrews lived on the opposite side of the street, and he was bitten by the Wireless bug. With bits and pieces, salvaged from goodness knows where, he had actually constructed his "set" on two shelves of his kitchen wall-cupboard. In the garden, a high flag-pole carried the copper ariel into the ether.

"It will be good tonight", he promised optimistically.

Dutifully at precisely 9 pm, I walked with my parents, across the road, to witness and share, this mind-blowing, 20th Century, experience. We found Willie pouring a jug of water over the outside earth-wire. "Improves performance", he explained, unnecessarily. Returning to the kitchen, he proudly opened the cupboard door, and we viewed the mess of the old valves, home- made coils, wires and batteries, with some apprehension.

A flick of a switch, and the valves glowed.

"She's ready now", beamed Willie. He fastened the earphones over his head, and slowly turned the tuning knob.

"Ah yes", he murmured to himself, obviously he had made contact with some being from outer space. My father, then my mother donned the earphones, but neither seemed impressed, then it was my turn.

Eagerly I clamped the "Brown" earphones over my head, but I can't

138

remember hearing any speech or music. Perhaps my hearing wasn't quite sensitive enough, who knows, somewhere in the crackles and howls, a form of intelligence, might be trying to get through.

My mother returned to No 22, with a face as long as a fiddle, then rounded on father, "That was a damn waste of time".

But the flame of desire had been kindled, secretly she yearned for one of those sets, advertised in newspapers, the ones with a built-in loudspeaker, and described grandiosely as a "Superhet".

A Wireless with a built-in speaker, could cost £6 or more. But mother set her sights a little higher, on a three valve "Mullard", at £8. This was far beyond our means, but the financial problem was soon to be solved by a local shopkeeper.

Ellis Polkinghorn was the proprietor of a small shop on Fore Street, catering for sweets, tobacco, and gent's barbering, at one time he also sold bicycles. Ellis decided to bring the Wireless to the masses, for the sum of just half-a-crown a week.

Suddenly, many houses in the street sported a Wireless, doors were left open, to see which was the loudest. Mother paid her half-a-crown and became the proud possessor of the "Mullard".

With no mains electricity, the power source had to be batteries.

The main dry battery was a 120 volt monster, glorifying in trade names, "Vidor", "Lucas", and Seimens "Full-O-Power", costing from four shillings for the German, to as much as seven and six for the English makes. But the volts didn't end there. One also needed a 9 volt grid-bias dry battery, and the inevitable 2 volt wet accumulator. Alas the accumulator had to be re-charged every 14 days at Horace Berry's, who operated a charging plant (at six-pence a time) from his house, in a lane aptly named, "Behind the Wall" at Ventonleague.

It was the large batteries that let us down. The sets played quite well for a few weeks, but by the end of the expected three months, even the National programme was just a squeak.

Radio Luxembourg was a bit of a strain, for our "Superhet", (even with new batteries) and on Sunday afternoons I sat with my ear glued to the loudspeaker, listening to, "Dr Fu Manchu", "Carson Robinson", and the "Ovaltinies". The wireless was most appreciated on Saturday evenings. First the news, then "In Town Tonight", followed by a variety show, and finishing with a mystery play. All from Britain's one and only National station.

There was little money in Hayle in the 1930s, even the shops just staggered on from week to week. Kate Jory sold very little, she had the same toys in her shop window, year after year.

The Government of the day considered that £5 a week was the minimum income that a family of four, could live on. Obviously they had never lived in Cornwall. My father, when in full employment, earned, as a carpenter, under £3 a week, fully trained and experienced engineers much less than that. As for the labourers just over £2 was the norm', Dick Toy wasn't getting that much in 1939.

The fact was, that the working class were not getting a healthy diet. The powers-to-be seemed to have woken up to the medical situation, and in the mid' 1930s introduced milk to the schools, at hap-penny a bottle (just under half a pint). The very poor, who couldn't afford the pittance, had theirs free. It was too late for many teenagers, their teeth had already turned grey, by the time they were old enough to vote, they would have lost them completely.

In the late 1920s, the noble art of dentistry was in the hands of our two chemists, Irvin P Moffat, and Ernest F Uren (Ernie). Fillings were unheard of, doubtful teeth were just yanked out.

It was a simple procedure. The victim sat in the chair while the dentist applied the miracle of medical science, guaranteed to alleviate all pain. A spot of cocain on a plug of cotton-wool, daubed ceremoniously on the gums, gave the patient a false sense of faith and security.

A few seconds later, the unfortunate had slid off the chair howling in agony, with the resolute practitioner still hanging on to the offending molar.

Ignoring the screams of his anguished patient, he finally stood up, proudly brandishing his grisly trophy.

"There you are, I told you it wouldn't hurt".

With a bloodied handkerchief clutched to his mouth, the recipient hurriedly paid his fee, and staggered blindly into the street.

"Next please", called out the ever optimistic artisan, but the waiting room had already emptied.

I was nine years old when I had my first extraction, at the school surgery. I suffered shock for hours after, but I suppose I could count myself lucky, because by this time Dentists had to be qualified. The school dentist that day came from Penzance, he should have stayed there.

In the meantime Ernie's son Kenneth (Kenny) had donned the mantle of Hayle's first qualified dentist, and remained thus enthroned for many, many years.

Between the two World Wars, there was a "Sick Benefit" of sorts, but it was subject to many "Ifs". Providing one met all the qualifying conditions, a princely sum of fifteen shillings per week was provided, for man and wife, children were not considered, there was nothing in the kitty for them.

Some of the desperately ill, struggled to work, when they should have been recuperating in bed.

My cousin, Bill Philp, who lived on the opposite side of the street, broke his ankle. With a wife and five children to support, there was no way he could stay at home to recuperate. So he tightly bound his ankle, and the next day cycled off to work. His job wasn't behind a desk, he worked with a pick and shovel. His eldest daughter, Stella, told me, "The bone set eventually, but the ankle was never the same again".

Leonard Alfred Weale was an employee at the Electric Works. His working life came to an abrupt end when he accidentally fell twenty feet, and he spent the next twenty-one years, bedridden. The works compensation helped at first, but when that ran out, it was "One day at a time" for his wife and two children, Douglas and Vera, every penny had to be accounted for.

Janie Kneebone was already crippled with arthritis, when she and her family came to live in the street, she moved along slowly, with the aid of a stick. The horse and cart arrived, her husband "Dick" and the three children, Rona, John, Beryl, carried the furniture indoors. When I first saw her, she was trying to help, by carrying an oil lamp. It is odd how these little details still stick in one's mind.

Over the following years, her health slowly deteriorated, until eventually, the arthritis and asthma took their toll, and Janie spent most of her waking life, in a chair. Her husband now had a full-time job, looking after her and the children. Janie helped as best she could, but it is not easy, washing the clothes, and kneading the dough, from the confines of a chair.

She spent her last years, as a helpless, bedridden cripple. During those years of torturous pain, I never heard her complain, or criticise another. She had an in-born sense of humour, and could tell a story, or turn a phrase, that would make the listener chuckle.

In 1948 she suffered a heart attack. The doctor called an ambulance, and Janie was hurried away to Redruth Hospital.

To everyone's surprise, she remarkably recovered, the devotional care of the nurses had reaped the reward. But there was one day she appeared to suffer a set-back, a nurse found her distressed and crying. The nurse tried to console her.

"Come along Mrs Kneebone, you've been doing so well, and be going home soon, what is it that's upsetting you so much?"

Janie dried her eyes and looked at the nurse.

"You've been so kind to me, I've had the most marvellous treatment and attention, since I've been here, but there's one thing you don't understand my dear, I haven't any money to pay for it".

Another nurse joined the bedside, and they stood looking at her and smiling.

"We've forgotten, you haven't heard the news have you".

"What news?"

"There's a National Health Service now, you don't have to pay for anything".

Thomas Cecil Hosking was wounded in World War 1. A bullet shattered his right knee, and a silver plate was fitted, his daughter, Marjorie, tells me that in the cold weather, the knee would open like a dog's mouth. Another bullet entered the front of his left foot, coming out underneath. I remember him having a lot of trouble with the fitted plugs. Bathing his wounds in salt water, seemed to give some relief, and Marjorie was frequently seen pilgrimaging to the dock, with a bucket, to fetch the sea-water.

When Cecil was hospitalised after being wounded, he was told that amputation was the only answer, but he stubbornly refused to be butchered in this fashion. The authorities immediately cancelled his "War wounded pension". Cecil's decision proved to be the right one, his wounded legs lasted him until he died, at the age of 80.

Tom Allen was born at St Ives, but lived in our street for some years during the 1930s. He volunteered for service in World War 1 when he was still only 18 (acceptance age was 19, but this wasn't questioned). His 19th birthday found him behind a machine gun on Vimy Ridge, then he moved to the Somme, and later Ypres. He was wounded in the neck, but after a time, returned to his unit. Tom luckily survived the bullets, shelling, and gas attacks. He married Emelene Kneebone, and they had a son, Barrie.

In the post-war years, work was spasmodic, and like many others, he decided to go to Canada for a few years, make some money, then return and hopefully buy a cottage for himself and family, (this was always in the mind of the emigrant).

Tom Allen
(photo: B. Allen)

After 5 years overseas, he returned and duly registered at the Labour Exchange, then his problems started. He was 5 years without "Stamps", and was curtly told, he had no claim to the Dole. He pointed out that he had served his country faithfully during the war, but his plea fell on deaf ears, the shutters came down. The voice of officialdom had only three words for his predicament,

"Too bad mate".

A tree felling enterprise came to an abrupt end, when he injured his hand. His Canadian nest egg dwindled away to almost nothing. Tom and his family won through, and he eventually found a permanent job, as a gardener.

Tom Allen never forgot, or forgave, the callous treatment of the authorities, and he never again accumulated enough money to buy the little cottage, he had always dreamed of.

In his moments of frustration and despair, his wife would quietly quote the 17th Century lines of Francis Quarles.

Our God and soldiers we alike adore,
Ev'n at the brink of danger, not before;
After deliverance, both alike requited,
Our God's forgotten, and our soldiers slighted.

23

Nothing sacred

Sending up the pompous, has always been a Cornish pastime.

Meetings addressed by the dignitaries, often ended in utter chaos, when someone inadvertently (with of course profuse apologies) mixed up the speech papers, or mislaid the presentation. Brass Bands were also ideal targets, and were not to escape the hook.

The tubular bell solo, in the middle of Ketelbey's "In a Monastery Garden", came over to the devoted, as just a succession of muted "dinks". The grass stuffed into the tubes, had performed admirably well. The Bandmaster was not pleased, Camborne Town Band never lived it down, and I happen to know the rotter who did it.

Of course, there was the ultimate disintegrator, and no Brass Band, however well disciplined, could withstand that horror.

A small group of lads stood directly in front of the musicians, and sucked lemons.

Long hours of dedicated practice with the "3rd Act from Lohengrin" dribbled (literally), into a garbled version of "I'm Forever Blowing Bubbles". I suppose one would have to be a band enthusiast, to appreciate the shame of such an exhibition.

Electioneering could not go without its moments of drama.

Workers in steady, and, more or less, safe jobs, were expected to vote Conservative. Those that didn't, kept a very low profile, because there was always a suspicion that the democratic process of secret voting, was a bit of a sham, and their jobs could be in jeopardy. Farm workers and Engineers worked for very low wages, unbelievably many helped to swell the "blue vote".

Building tradesmen, like my father, were paid a little more. Constantly on the move, from one job to another, they considered themselves politically independent, and gave no allegiance to anyone. Invariably they voted for the candidate who represented a shiv-in-the-gut to the established system. In groups they talked darkly about the great rising, soon to come. I never heard the word "Communism", instead they went all the way back to the French Revolution, "Bring out the tumbrels" and "To the guillotine", was the cry. I had this awful apprehension, that when the New World finally dawned, only the people of St John's Street, would still be around to witness it.

There were of course, still some staunch Liberals dotted about, and the beleaguered Labour Party, trying to get its act together, after a rather futile attempt at Government.

The Labour Party brought Kate Spurrel down to Hayle, to try and inject some enthusiasm into the flagging voter. She certainly did that. During one of her rousing speeches, she lifted the hem of her skirt, to show her pink knickers, shouting, "I'm red all through".

The women spectators were shocked into silence, but the opposite sex cheered her to a man.

As usual, the Tory won, and was towed by some of the underlings through the town, his Eminence standing in the open polished conveyance, waving and smiling triumphantly to the minions.

It was the last we were to see, or hear of him, until the next election. Father, who had voted for Kate, simply muttered, "good riddance", and went home.

> Confound their politics,
> Frustrate their knavish tricks,
> On thee our hopes we fix,
> God save us all.
> Part verse from our National Anthem (now deleted).

Motor Tax was on a rising scale, the higher the horse-power, the more tax one had to pay. Cars for the working class were practically unknown, but a few did roar around on motor cycles, which had seen better days.

One chap managed to partially solve the horse-power problem, he fitted a 500cc engine, to a 350cc frame. Not that the motor tax was a worry to him, he never paid any, I often saw him bumping his noisy steed through the street, proudly displaying behind the yellowing celluloid of his tax disc holder, a "Bass" label.

My father had always claimed, that he had never earned enough to pay Income Tax, and naturally never bothered with tiresome tax forms.

Long after he retired, he received a letter from the Newcastle tax office. They had painstakingly ploughed through the files, of his working life, and found, he had in fact, cheated them.

In no uncertain terms, the seriousness of the offence was rammed home. A criminal act had been committed, and if the debt was not settled immediately, shameful retribution would surely follow. Father had visions of being flogged and hung from the yard-arm, he admitted defeat, and reluctantly sent off the postal order. A whole £2, the year was 1960.

However, he cheered up a bit, when he realised, it must have cost the tax office a small fortune, just checking him up.

The "Royals" seldom visited Cornwall, probably the Imperial warning bells had sounded, and they feared what pit-falls lay in wait. The classic example happened in the Scilly Isles, when the Prince of Wales (later to be the Duke of Windsor) visited those fair climes.

Arthur (Painter) Martin, was in the islands at that time, working on a building site.

The coming of the Prince, was an occasion not to be missed, the dignitaries and the more prosperous business men, with their patronising smiles, lined the quayside, to await His Royal Highness.

The solitary resident policeman on St Mary's was now backed up by a contingent from the mainland, their sole purpose, to keep the "scruffs" well in the rear, and out of mischief.

The great moment arrived, the Prince walked down the gang-plank, and had just set foot on the quay, when it happened.

Arthur suddenly pushed himself to the front, taking off his cap, he made a stiff bow, and in a loud voice proclaimed,

"Welcome your Majesty".

It wasn't exactly the correct term of address, but that didn't seem to worry the Prince, he took it all in his stride, and without hesitation, shook Arthur's hand. For the next few minutes they stood talking to each other, he asked Arthur his name and what he did for a living, the painter responded by telling him what life was like, on the other side of the fence. The Prince listened intently to all that was said, but couldn't suppress a smile when he looked across at "God's gift to mankind", and saw their faces purple with shame and indignation.

At six o-clock that evening, Arthur was back in his lodgings, enjoying his tea, when a knock was heard. Opening the door, he found a messenger boy with a sealed letter, from the Island's council. Arthur signed for the letter and read it aloud at the table.

The actual words have not been passed on, but the gist of it was this.

147

"Because of your disgraceful and unseemly conduct with the Prince of Wales this afternoon, you will leave the Islands with the next sailing of the S. S. Scillonian, and never, never, return again".

Arthur took his deportation philosophically, and over the years, often referred to the Prince of Wales as a "Nice sort of chap".

Pulpit mishaps are legend in Cornwall, many of them still told today.

Local preacher Willie Web (a massive powerful man with a voice to match) was expounding the "Word", with loud and fearful deliberation, when suddenly his false teeth flew out, and disappeared into the depths beyond. He quickly left the rostrum, and after a frantic search, retrieved his precious dentures from under the communion rail. Checking to ensure that all was well, he popped them back in, and returned to the pulpit. Glaring the irreverent titterers into silent submission, he continued with his sermon. Alas the spell was broken, the carefully prepared "Word", soon forgotten. Not so, the story of the errant teeth, for that story lived forever on.

This chapter would not be complete, without a mention of Solly Stone, and I am indebted to George Williams for this anecdote.

Solly was a devout Methodist Preacher, one of the "Old school". Prophecy of Armageddon and retribution for the unrepented, blasted forth from the pulpit with devotional furiosity. He was, unfortunately, prone to mishaps, and this alone was enough to endear him to the Cornish congregations. Only a character of his standing and wit, could turn an impending disaster, into a personal triumph.

His near downfall could not be attributed to the whim of a prankster, he had his own Achilles Heel, an insatiable appetite for – rhubarb tart –

He was taking the service at Ventonleague Chapel, when his aplomb collapsed. In the middle of the first hymn, he raised his arms, the singing stopped, and a hush fell over all.

"My friends, this evening I had tea with Grace Ann Penberthy, and couldn't resist a piece of her rhubarb tart. I love rhubarb tart, but it doesn't like me. So my friends I must leave you for a few minutes, but keep on singing friends, keep on singing, for I shall return".

Ventonleague Chapel. 1952

After a time Solly returned to the pulpit, and continued with the service. Then, during another hymn, his hands again flew heavenward, and a hush once more quietened the Chapel.

"My friends, it's happened again, nature calls and I must away,
but keep on singing friends, keep on singing, for I shall return".

These wonderful characters are no longer with us, and Cornwall is a much sorrier place with their passing.

I never heard Solly Stone preach, but then, as a lad, I never attended a service at a chapel. But at times when I stand alone in Ventonleague Chapel, it seems as if his presence is still there. His battle cry echoing faintly through the rafters, "Keep on singing friends, for I shall return". And in my mind's eye, I see the congregation happily responding in perfect harmony.

"Hold the fort, for I am coming".

149

24

Creatures littler than thou

Animals, as pets, were accepted around the houses, but we never had a dog, a licence of seven shillings and sixpence per year, was considered a stone-around-the-neck, in the 1930s. Still there were a few about, "Sport", an over-fed spaniel of my cousin Bill, spent most of his waking life with the young toddlers of the street. Mrs Lang's terrier, "Peter" had a devilish sense of humour, he peered into the street, from the sanctuary of his gateway, then spotting a loose ball, scurried into the street, snapped up the ball and scampered back to No 24. Howls of anguish soon brought Kate Lang to the rescue, and the reluctant animal, still clutching his catch, was dragged struggling, from its lair under the kitchen table.

In a moment of unprecedented benevolence, my father promised me a dog. But I didn't take too much notice of this wild promise. He meant well, but as usual, the seed of his good intent, fell on stoney ground. The small dog was a gift, he tucked it under his coat, and then attempted to cycle with it from Lelant, a distance of over two miles. When the animal escaped the second time, he gave up.

A few "Commyack" pigeons, flew in and out of a small shed, at the top of the garden. (The name Commyack was given to birds of doubtful parentage, usually a mixed breed of Homers and Tumblers). These feathered friends were mostly fed on wheat, at a penny a pound, purchased from George Hammond's the corn chandler, in Market Square. During the winter, the more expensive kibble maize was added to their diet. "Keeps them warm during the cold spells", we were told. To get a real nice gloss in the neck feathers, a little hemp seed was introduced. The pigeons went mad to get at this, I suppose it acted like a drug. Some hemp seed, found its way outside the wire-netting, and a fair crop of hemp, continually sprouted, in wild confusion. Everyone was aware that if smoked, it could become addictive, but no one ever did, the people in the street had too much common sense for such

150

nonsense. At regular intervals, it was dug up, and burned on the garden bonfire.

For a time we kept bantams, instead of pigeons, but therein lay a mystery. The bantam eggs kept on disappearing at an alarming rate. It was a situation that could not go on unchecked, the culprit must meet his comeuppence.

Father donned his investigator badge, and decided to track down the marauder. The half-starved cats that roamed the gardens, were easily eliminated from the scene of the crime, by more security, namely, sealing off all holes that could give access, and repairing rotting timbers. Still the eggs disappeared, and only the rats that infested the tops of the gardens, remained the obvious answer. But the investigator could not understand how a rat could get an egg down a hole, barely large enough for its own body to squeeze into.

For more than a hour, that Sunday, he sat on a wooden box, staring through a hole he had bored through the poultry house door. Two rats came out of hiding, one of them approached the nest and carried off the egg in its front paws. Nearing the hole it turned on its back, still firmly holding the egg. The other rat grabbed at the inviting tail, with its teeth, then slowly backed down the hole, dragging its toboggan with him. Father could hardly believe what he had seen, but having witnessed the cunning ploy, he now decided to relinquish his investigator role, and turn exterminator.

There were a number of guns available from our neighbours, but the chosen weapon was a single barrelled shotgun pistol. Squinting along the barrel, he had a rather restricted view through the top of the hole, but it was sufficient. The hunter pushed a .410 long cartridge into breech, and stuck the end of the barrel through the hole, and awaited the quarry. In the meantime, mother and I retired to the kitchen. "Better leave him be", she said.

How long he sat in ambush, on that apple box, is anybody's guess, but, much, much, later, a loud explosion echoed from the garden. Hurrying to the scene of battle, we found the exterminator flat on his back, nursing, what soon would be, the daddy of all black- eyes. He had once again forgotten the golden rule, "never fire a gun in a garden", he had also forgotten that these pistols kicked like a mule. Holding one of these guns close to the eye, for aiming, was hardly the sensible thing to do.

Oblivious to any pain from his rapidly closing optic, he proudly proclaimed, "I got um, both of um". Opening the shed door, we stared in disbelief at the carnage. At only four feet he just couldn't miss, and with a choke barrel, there was only a minimum spread of shot. An unrecognisable mess of ripped flesh, bone and sinew, lay on the earthen floor. The exterminator gleefully poked a stick down the hole and retrieved the other unfortunate. It was a sorry sight, one side of the animal was torn completely away.

The "League of Vermin" must have got the message, organised egg raids, ceased from that day. The episode also taught me a lesson. I had seen rabbits shot at a distance, with little disfigurement, but until now, I had never known what devastation a shotgun could deliver at close quarters.

It was a warm clear night, when I heard it. A faint cry of a baby, from the garden hedge. It wasn't a baby, I knew that cry for help. A hedgehog was being attacked by a voracious rat. Once heard, never forgotten, the cry seems unnatural and eerie. I've heard this cry only twice during my lifetime, the second time was at Ventonleague, many years later. The hedgehog was rescued, and kept for a few days in a shed, on a diet of bread and milk. With its wounds healing, it was released again into the wild.

Uncle Dick had worked for a time in Burma, he told me that a wounded monkey would cry like a baby. Although he had hunted many different animal species in his time, including a tiger, (which incidentally got away) he could never bring himself to shoot a monkey, not after hearing that cry.

We were chatting one day at the side of the road, when a girl walked by, with a monkey on her shoulder. "She's making a big mistake", he said, "they never make good pets and are very destructive, better leave them in the wild, or put them in a Zoo".

He probably never warned Stanley Cox, for Stanley had a monkey, kept for most of the time, in an outside cage, but occasionally allowed the freedom of the house. Family heirlooms on the mantlepiece, were swept to destruction, curtains were ideal for climbing, and thereby suffered considerably. Nothing was sacred, yet when my parents visited the Cox's, the animal behaved itself impeccably. But then father helped to some extent, by allowing the furry beast to sit on his shoulder, pulling and thoroughly inspecting every hair on his head.

Alas the primate blotted its copybook, when given the freedom of the garden. It grabbed a rooster by its legs, and scurried to the top of a clothes pole. Totally oblivious to Stanley's rage, and his threatening clothesprop, it proceeded to de-plume, the suspended, protesting bird, feather by feather, finally letting the poor nude, and now flightless creature, fall to the ground with a bump.

Queenie, was our cat, a long haired skinny feline, born in my year, 1924.

"She's a d . . . thief", said mother, after seeing the hungry animal stick a paw into a milk jug, and then lick it clean. The cat and I were good friends, when mother dismissed my knee abrasions (and there were many) with an unsympathetic, "It will soon be alright, nothing to worry about", it was Queenie who did her best, to clean the wound. I rewarded her with the corner of my pasty, if the grown-ups were looking the other way, with, if available, a little milk to follow. Tinned animal food was unheard of, in those days, we couldn't afford it, even if it was. Many domestic pets had a lean time, a few scraps from the table, if they were lucky, had to suffice. Vets, what were they? I never saw or heard of them, as for medication, I can only assume that the worms outlived the animals. Some of the older men forced their dogs to swallow a sliver of tobacco, claiming it had remarkable cleansing properties, a positive cure for worms, they were probably right.

Terminally sick dogs were usually shot. Cats, too ill to care, and unwanted kittens, were condemned to a sack, plunged into a bucket of water, and weighted down with a stone on top, until they drowned. Squeamish neighbours begged father to be executioner, he hated doing it, but obliged rather than they mess it up. It was something that had to be done, the way of the street.

Queenie lived to the ripe old age of 13. She had developed a strange black growth, covering the front bottom teeth, so much so, it was all she could do to lap milk, let alone eat anything solid. In desperation the animal tore the "thing" from her gums, and for a short time, seemed to recover, but it was a losing battle, the "thing" started growing again. Father examined a piece of the torn growth, under a student's bisecting microscope, (a find from the Launceston College tip) he was surprised to discover that the growth was matted fur rooted to the gums. In later years, I asked a number of vets about this, but none could give an explanation.

Slowly Queenie lost the flight, her strength sapped away, spending most of the daytime, sleeping in the sunshine, on the lavatory roof, easily reached from the adjoining garden hedge. One afternoon, weak and hardly able to stand, she slid off the roof, and into the courtyard.

Mother now sadly, had to do the inevitable.

There was to be, no bucket, no bag, no stone. A small bath of luke-warm water was prepared in the kitchen. She picked Queenie up, the animal didn't struggle, just looked at her as if to say, "Do it now".

She placed the animal in the bath, and with just one hand, gently held its head beneath the water.

I watched until the air bubbles were no more, and a little bit of me died with her.

25

The quiet man

Doctor Palmer glared over the top of his pince-nez, father stood in trepidation before the learned man.

"Contrary to my instructions, I have seen you riding a cycle to work".

Father murmured sheepishly, something about, "having to earn a living".

"Dead men do not earn a living", spat out the medic. "You have a blood clot in that leg, if that clot moves, it could be a wooden box for you. Good God! Philp, you know what you have to do, you've done it before, and if I see you on that bike again, I shall cross your name from my patient list".

Father groaned inwardly, six weeks in bed, and a sick benefit of fifteen shillings a week, was not something to be looked forward to.

He had been caught cycling to work, some three miles away, at Gwinear Road railway station. His ulcerated legs started bleeding with the effort, the blood running down and dripping into his boots. Every day he paused en route, a kindly district nurse tightly bandaged his wounds, hopefully enabling him to work for the rest of the day. By the time he returned home in the evening, his legs were a mess. Mother bathed his legs with elder tea, it seemed to give some relief. He didn't tell Dr Palmer, that at one time he was cycling as far as Paul Hill, Newlyn, a distance of twelve miles from home base. If the good doctor had known, he would probably have thrown in the towel, without hesitation. Father was left with no choice, and retired to his bed.

Every other day I walked the street, tapping on doors, imploring the kind neighbours to lend me a few of their American pulp magazines, in an effort to relieve father's boredom. Willie Andrews and Leonard Morris were both avid readers of the "Pulps", and obliged on a number of occasions. But six weeks is a long, long, time.

Mother managed quite well, financially, when father was working, but he was often confined to his sick bed. To off-set this certain

155

eventuality, she put a few shillings aside each week, for the inevitable day.

We could just about get by on the dole. If the breadwinner was expected to be ill for only a week, he struggled to the dole office on the Monday, signed the dotted line, then back to his bed. On Saturday (pay-day) I was the chosen one to collect.

"If anyone asks any awkward questions, tell them your father is out looking for a job". But no-one ever asked, I had a feeling they knew, but turned a blind eye to it. This conn' could not be worked indefinitely, mother supplemented the sick benefit, with many dips into the money-box. At the end of three weeks, the cupboard was bare.

Father was feeling much better, and, against doctors orders, walking about the house, and even into the garden.

"If I could only get a light job", he kept on repeating, "two or three hours a day would help".

But light jobs there were none, a partial cripple was hardly at the top of the employment stakes, and the beady, omnipresent eye of the Doctor, effectively curbed all cycling espeditions to the far fields.

Once again it was the "Day of the Sops". But at that time, none of us gave a thought to the "Quiet man".

Mr Cann and his wife purchased a grocery business in Market Square, from the retiring Oliver's. Cann was a naval reservist, always the polite gentleman, I never heard him raise his voice. My mother had been purchasing our groceries from Cann's shop for some time, and often referred to him as a "nice quiet man".

Our weekly grocery bill was settled on the Saturday. This was the norm, because Saturday was the traditional pay-day.

On this particular day, our total grocery bill was just a few shillings, having bought only the very basic requirements. The shopkeeper called mother to one side, and in his quiet way remonstrated with a few home truths.

"I've watched you these last few weeks, and I know you haven't been buying enough for yourself and family".

Mother simply replied, "It's all I could afford, Mr Cann". The shopkeeper had no intention of being brushed aside, and relentlessly continued,

"In future you must take all you need, pay me again at some later date", and then he added, "If you can't, don't worry, I'll never raise the question again".

Mother, stubborn to the last, thanked him for his kind offer, and murmured, "It will be alright, we'll manage – somehow".

I suppose most shopkeepers would give up at this stage, but Cann was made of sterner stuff.

At 6 o'clock that evening, I answered a knock at the door. Standing on the doorstep, was the lad from the shop, with an important letter for Mr. Philp. Father retired to the kitchen with the envelope, hardly knowing what to think. He read the contents aloud at the table.

– "A light job was available at the shop – a few minor repairs – two hours a morning would suffice – if he was interested".

It was the light at the end of the tunnel. Father happily spent Sunday morning sharpening his tools, this was what he was looking for, and less than five minutes walk from home. With luck he could dodge the doctor's all-seeing eye.

Prompt at 8.30 on Monday morning, he presented himself at the shop. The shopkeeper and his wife arrived a few minutes later.

"Overslept this morning", yawned Cann, "came away without our breakfast, not to worry, we'll put the kettle on and all have a cup of tea".

The last thing the carpenter wanted, was tea, he had downed his breakfast, bread and milk, only fifteen minutes before. Still the boss had spoken, tea it had to be. Father curbed his impatience as best he could, but it was some time before Cann presented him with his first job, – replacing a small cracked window pane, at the rear of the premises –

It was obvious that the glass had cracked many, many, years before, and the carpenter couldn't understand the sudden urgency. He replaced the pane, and gave the window frame a much needed coat of paint, then reported back to his benefactor, but by this time the shopkeeper had decided it was time for another cuppa.

Suitably refreshed, and after some deliberation, Cann offered up his next job. A piece of floorboard was to be taken up and inspected for suspect dry-rot. It looked alright to father, but he cut out the indicated flooring, only to find (as expected) there was nothing wrong with it, exasperated he relaid it.

After another cup of tea, father's two hours of duty had expired, and a very bemused but happy carpenter returned to No 22.

And so, each day, the farce was played, for some unknown reason, he never caught on, not even when he found more in his pay packet than expected. All his life he had worked for employers who wanted every "drop of blood", it wouldn't occur to him that he was a pawn in the gentle art of christian charity.

Mother bought the groceries she required, and was able to pay for all.

All good things must come to an end, after his six weeks total "convalescence", Dr Palmer declared him fit for work, and lived forever in ignorance of the shop venture. Father thanked Mr Cann for the job, and duly signed on at the Labour Exchange.

It was some months later, father had finished his tea and was sitting by the kitchen table, deep in thought, with the cat on his lap.

Mother looked at him, "What are you grinning at Leonard?"

"Nothing much", he replied, "just thinking about ole Cann, funny sort of chap, I didn't naw 'e wus so eccentric, hardly any work to do, spent most of my time drinking tea, softest job I ever 'ad, and on top of it all, 'e overpaid me". He paused, and then added, "Still it worked out alright fer us, don't naw how we would have managed without it".

Suddenly the smiled dropped from his face, he looked at mother, and then in mock anger, "The ole devil, 'e 'ad me on, didn't 'e?"

Mother nodded, "He fooled the both of us Leonard".

They were still laughing together, when I went out to play.

Cann was recalled into the navy, when hostilities were imminent in 1939. Soon after his wife closed the shop, and it was taken- over by the engineering company J & F Pool Ltd, for use as an office.

The last I heard, the Canns had set up home in Falmouth, and although I never saw them again, I never forgot,

"The Quiet Man".

– the greatest of these is charity.
1. Corinthians 13:13.

26

A story to tell

On a fine day, the men gathered in small groups at the "Bridge" or "Cornubia" corner, usually on a Sunday morning, and swopped their oft-told stories.

Edmund Mitchel, a first class blacksmith, worked most of his life in the shipyard. He remembered the "Lead Rivet" fiasco, a little bit of Hayle's inglorious past that is never written about in the authoratative tomes of the town's historical past.

"The profit margin was running low in the shipyard, so they imported the clever-dicks from Bristol, a belated effort to set the business back on a sound financial footing. Soft rivets were introduced to speed up production. We called them "Lead Rivets".

The completed ship steamed out of Hayle harbour, and into St Ives bay, for her trials, leaked like a basket and almost fell apart. Luckily they got her back in one piece, but it cost a fortune to put her right. It was the beginning of the end, for Hayle shipyard.

Barns Wright had a story to tell. He was a big (six foot two in his socks) man, hard and merciless.

In 1939 I found myself working alongside him in the Moulding Shop. During morning "crowst" I casually mentioned America, that was all that was required to get the story teller talking.

He finished munching his saffron bun, spat into the black sand floor, obviously delighted to have a listener.

"I went to America twice, the last time I travelled across the states, and down to Mexico, worked in the silver mines there. Not bad for a chap who couldn't read or write. They had money problems, Cornish- men were brought in to try and get the mine profitable, and I was one of them. We worked the old way, taking over parts of the mine, buying our own tools and blasting sticks, more or less treating the venture as our own business, being paid only by results. Pushing ourselves to the limit, with long hours and hard work, we did exceptionally well, but the Mexican workers, with less than half our pay, were in a belligerent mood. Fights often broke out. One particular Mex' threatened me many times. "One day beeg Gringo, I stick thees in you". He pulled a large, razor sharp, Bowie knife from his belt, and made a cut- throat gesture. I knew he meant it, and I knew that one day soon, it would be him or me. He didn't know it, but he threatened the wrong man, I had already decided that it wasn't going to be me. A few days later we were working near each other, and I realised there was no one else within earshot. I crept up behind him, he instinctively sensed danger, but he was too late, I grabbed him, lifted him off his feet, and hurled him down a stope. No one ever saw him again".

He paused, and then as an afterthought he said.

"You know boy, I can't ever remember hearing him call out".

In the distance a bell sounded, we fastened our "crowst" bags, and returned to the core making.

(Barns Wright is a pseudonym)

Mrs Gibson, on the opposite side of our street, sold a few sweets, pop and tea from her front room window, it helped to eke out the pension. Her husband was a chronic asthmatic, and often I have looked through the doorway into their kitchen, to see him, his head covered with a towel, leaning over a bowl of hot steaming water and Friars Balsam, breathing the vapour, in a vain effort to get some relief.

But who would have thought that little Mrs Gibson (she couldn't have been more than five feet tall) had her share of drama, in her younger days.

"I was living in Mexico during the revolution. There was a lot of gunfire in the streets, and we were told to stay clear of the doors and windows. I remember peering around the corner of a window and seeing some rebels running across the roop-tops. The Federals stood in the street, and shot them off the ridges. I don't think any escaped, it all looked so unreal, as if they were shooting in a fairground".

She told me this, and other stories, when I was still a young teenager, at that time I took no notes, it never occurred to me, that one day I might write a little of her story.

She had a son, and fostered others. One was a foundling, with no name, the street never lacking in ingenuity, christened him "Commons".

I cannot recall the actual dates of her Mexico story, history tells us that the revolution dragged on from 1910 to 1917.

I liked the lamp-light stories best of all. In the depths of winter, the men gathered in the kitchen. I can see them now, their faces barely lit by the single-burner oil lamp on the table, and the glow from the open fire-doors of the Slab. I was still a young lad, and I sat mute in the corner, and listened in wonderment to their tales of adventure, avarice, and guile.

Uncle Dick and Uncle Will voiced their contribution, they had worked together at the Anaconda Mines of Butte, Montana, and served as Deputy Sheriffs for a time.

"On pay night we stopped on our way home and had a drink at the 'Ramada' in Butte. One night we were celebrating as usual, when the bat-wing door flew open, and in walked three armed men, their faces masked by their bandannas. 'Put em up', they snapped. Well you don't argue when looking down the barrels of three .45s, so we obediently raised our arms. One of the bandits walked around the saloon, taking our money belts, loose change, and anything else of value, then tipping the plunder into a hessian sack, followed by the contents of the cash register. The bartender was ordered to fill up all the glasses. With guns still pointed, they slowly backed away, when they reached the swing doors, the leader of the bunch (who seemed to have a wry sense of humour) laughed and said, 'Have a drink on us when we're gone boys'. The quickly assembled posse, found nothing. We would have hung the s . . . if we had caught them, but Butte City is in the Rocky mountains, and only thing you ever catch there, is pneumonia".

Stories of poaching were always good for a few chuckles. A favourite territory for exploitation was the Squire Tyringhams estate at Lelant. Not only rabbits, but pheasant and chickens (domestic variety) abounded there. Gamekeeper Post tore his hair out, trying to catch the villains, but to no avail.

161

A rookie policeman from St Erth (hungry for promotion) decided to emulate Wyatt Earp, and personally round up the offenders.

Night after night he hid in ambush by the causeway, then one night the vigilance paid off – well almost –

The three innocents sauntered along the moonlit road, without a care in the world. Carrying their traps and nets wrapped in sacking, with a ferret tucked in an inside coat pocket. The truncheon bearing apparition that suddenly manifested itself, affected a sudden stop.

"Got you at last", shrilled the hopeful rookie, "Poachers, that's what you are".

The three stared with some amusement at Wyatt, who was already wishing he was somewhere else.

"Let's tip 'im over the wall", suggested one, hopefully.

"'it the silly ole fool on the 'ead", said another.

But the leader of the pack, summed up the situation with a little more foresight and compassion.

" 'ees only a little boy, ignor 'im".

So they pushed the protesting custodian of the law to one side, and continued on their way. Looking back a few moments later, to see a ghostly moonlit figure, furiously peddling his cycle towards Hayle.

" 'ees fergot to light his carbide lamp", said the leader, "I shall 'ave to report 'im to the law".

A convincing cover-up was now essential, poaching that night was definitely off.

They climbed down to the mud flats and cached their traps and nets, under some stones. An old wooden box was found for the ferret, and the creature was imprisoned just above the high water mark, hopefully it would still be there, when they could return, the next day.

They hung around for an hour, then casually walked back to Hayle, and the inevitable confrontation.

As expected, the police trap exploded in Foundry Square.

"Stay where you are", shouted the police sergeant suddenly appearing from nowhere, backed up by five others. The innocents stood meekly as ordered.

"Now", continued the sergeant, "we know you've been over to the Tyringham estate, and you've been poaching, so try to wriggle out of that if you can".

"You're wrong serg'", replied the leader, "we've only been down on the mud".

"And what", he asked, "have you been doing on the mud-flats at one-o-clock in the morning?"

"Gitting bait fer termarrow's fishing Serg'".

The speaker held up a rusty tin to prove his point. The sergeant took the proffered tin-can, put his hand inside, and withdrew the evidence – a piece of damp sea-weed – . He was hardly fooled by this obvious subterfuge, handing back the tin he growled, "Bait is it? you lying s . . . the only bait you ever caught had fur on it".

The police spent many uncomfortable nights on the causeway, a forlorn hope that they might catch the miscreants, but to no avail. The poaching continued unabaited, the "innocents" had found another route.

It had been a rough night, the rain pouring down in bucketfuls, but had eased somewhat just before day-break. An old rowing boat nosed its way (almost noiselessly) across the river from Lelant to Hayle. The goodly snare of rabbit and game, not forgetting a few vegetable delights, to complement the Sunday table, had made the trip worthwhile. The three boatmen (reasonably dry under their oilskins) paused in the middle of the harbour and stared at the wall of gloom between themselves and the causeway.

"Poor ole serg'," murmured the leader, with feigned sorrow, "must be wet through", then with a sudden burst of christian charity and compassion he said, "tell ee wot boys, I'll drop a rabbit on 'is doorstep on the way 'ome".

The fields around St Erth also offered prime pickings to the nocturnal adventurers, but necessitated another safe and easy way home. When I asked the leader, why they always returned via the same route, he simply grinned, cocked an eyebrow and said, "Ah boy! you'll never find a policeman on a railway line".

– Come to think of it, he's right –

When all the actors had long retired, the serg' often popped in to visit his old adversary. He was always greeted with good natured profanity. Then like old and forgotten warriors, they settled in the armchairs, smoked their pipes-of-peace, and for a few precious moments, relived their old battles all over again.

> "I will not want, when I have,
> nor by God, when I haven't too".
> Old Cornish Proverb.

163

27

Coming soon

For just tuppence, the boys and girls could go to the cinema on a Saturday afternoon, and for two-and-a-half hours or more, sit and enjoy a fascinating experience of make-believe, forgetting the mundane troubles of the outside world. Those who couldn't afford the admission, listened in rapture, as their more fortunate friends retold the stories, scene by scene.

As early as 1905 "Hancock's Living Pictures" or "Bioscope" as they were often called, was a feature at Truro Fair, but I can find no reference to it ever visiting Hayle. Few Hayle people could afford the thruppence admission, in 1905.

In the early years of the 1900s, professional entertainment was limited to the rare appearance of travelling players, specialising in the (already dated) Victorian melodramas, such as, "Sweeney Todd" and "Maria Marten" played with much gusto, to an enthralled and captivated audience, in the hastily converted little theatre – the barn behind the Commercial Hotel.

The first moving pictures (of sorts) my parents ever saw was, "Pools Panorama", a feature at many fairgrounds in the early days. It was simply a number of scenes (usually famous disasters) painted on a series of large screens, moving across the stage on rollers, accompanied by a cacophany of background noises and lighting effects, skillfully applied by the attendants hidden off-stage. I never saw the "Panorama", it had vanished before I was born, but despite competition from the films, it survived until the outbreak of World War 1. My parents remember "The Sinking of the Titanic" on the Panorama, and thought the illusion was terrific. The Titanic went to her watery grave in 1912.

But the age of the Cinema had dawned, overnight the Panorama and the Players, sank into obscurity.

The "Picturedome" was located at Foundry Square, on the first floor of the Public Hall.

Hancock's Living Pictures. Truro. Circa 1905)

Local business man Howard Pool was the proprieter, and the wonderful films of the 1920s were shown to enthusiastic audiences.

For the grand opening, the Hollywood production "Down to the Sea in Ships" was chosen, with Clara Bow in her first starring role. This film was made in 1922, but these little cinemas usually waited a long time for the releases, so it is reasonably safe to assume, that the actual first showing, at the "Picturedrome" would be 1923 or 1924. These approximate dates are confirmed by Lt. Cdr E. R. Coombe RN, who was about eight years old at the time.

On the opening night, he and three other choir-boys from Phillack Church, stood in front of the screen and sang, "Eternal father strong to save", accompanied by Rhoda Andrews on piano and violinist Monique Pool. This redoubtable musical duo, were very good musicians, and on that night and many more to follow, they constituted the "Pit orchestra". Later, Kathleen Dale at times, substituted as pianist.

No-one seems to know when the cinema closed, but the older boys told us about the extraordinary German Fritz Lang film, they had seen there. "Metropolis" was released in 1926, and most likely shown at the "Picturedrome", one or two years later.

Sadly for financial reasons, the cinema had to close. Probably with the "Talkies" looming large on the horizon, the extra running cost would not be justified. All we can be sure of is, that when the building was completely destroyed by fire, in 1935, the "Picturedrome" was already, just a receding memory.

But closer to home, at our end of the town (Copperhouse) a cinema had been established for some time, and was to flourish for more than 60 years.

In Market Square, the very old and dilapidated lock-ups, were pulled down, and a block of buildings erected. The cinema was incorporated on the upper floor, with shops underneath at ground level. A local builder, George Bond, was responsible for this complex. The shops were framed with green tiles, but overhead, the frontage of the cinema sported fawn tiles, culminating in a Georgian facade, over the abutments and to the apex. The projection box, cantilevered out from the frontage, proudly proclaiming the grandiose name, "St Georges Hall, 1914".

Into this tiny refuge, two "Simplex" projectors were installed. They were hand-cranked, the shutter resembled a fan and revolved in the open, just in front of the lens. Woe betide any unfortunate who trapped his fingers in that devilish contraption, but luckily, as far as I know, no-one ever did.

In the early silent days, the only background music was via a piano, ably performed with much fortitude by Gladys Wills.

I was five years old when I saw my first movie. A special showing for the school children, at 4 pm after class. For just one penny each, the whole school had been invited to see the silent classic, "Ben Hur", starring Ramon Navarro and Francis X Bushman.

The great day arrived, and we marched in military fashion, from the school to the cinema. In Market Square, we were banded into groups, and ushered up the long flight of steps, I handed my precious penny to the lady behind the glass panel, and stepped, for the very first time, into the auditorium.

It was actually, very, very, small indeed, (some locals called it, "The Cardboard Box") but to me it looked frighteningly large. I stared about in some trepidation, those two glass chandeliers, hanging from the ceiling, didn't look too safe, so, if I could, I would avoid sitting under those. I needn't have worried, I found myself sitting on a form at the very front, the teachers had, of course, comfortably ensconced themselves at the rear of the cinema, in the posh tip-ups.

With my head strained at about forty-five degrees, I looked at the yellowing screen. The cinema boasted no curtains in those days, but there was a picture-frame-like surround decorated with a celluloid frieze. I was intrigued with the Cherub cameo, at the top centre, holding some sort of drape, to cover his naughty bits. The Cherub seemed to have become partially unstuck, and in danger of falling off, but it remained in that precarious position, throughout the 1930s. I stared at the Cherub and the screen, waiting for the great moment.

Suddenly the lights dimmed, a few advertising slides were first projected, these were crudely drawn on sooted glass, by the operator, who obviously had no artistic talent. For only one penny we could hardly expect a full supporting programme, so it was straight into "Ben Hur".

I vaguely remember a background of music and effects, and as there was no visible piano, I concede there must have been a recorded disc of sound effects, issued with the picture.

As for the film itself (2 3/4 hours long) I found the experience far too trying for my tender years. When finally I was again released into the sunshine, I suffered a splitting headache and a very stiff neck. The only scenes I could recall, was a hazy recollection of galley slaves, and two ships ramming each other. I had forgotten the rest of the film, even the famous chariot race, and today, clips of this film classic on TV stir no hidden memories.

It must have been the eighth wonder of the world. The talking picture had, at last, arrived. St Georges had not yet taken the plunge, but five miles away at St Ives, the die had been cast.

My parents, now caught up in the general excitement, surreptitiously raided the tin money box hidden in the corner of the wall cupboard, and on the Saturday afternoon, disappeared for a few hours.

They had gone to St Ives to see their very first talkie – Ronald Colman in "Bulldog Drummond" – released by United Artists in 1929 (probably shown at St Ives in 1930). But with their ears battered by the crackles and scratches of that early sound equipment, the experience proved to be a nightmare.

Much later they both returned, looking strained and tired with mother complaining bitterly of a ranting headache, as she usually did when things went wrong. I smiled to myself, as I listened to their tale of woe. Serve them damn well right, I thought, for leaving me behind.

St Georges finally succumbed to the ever-growing popularity of the "Talkies". The "Simplex" projectors were up-dated, electric motors fitted, and room found for the necessary amplifier. Still giving yeoman service, the brass mounted "Magic Lantern" was squashed in the corner, advertising slides would be projected on that machine, for many more years to come.

The early "Talkies were sound-on-disc, and even after the introduction of sound-on-film, some movies were still being projected with a SOD recording, and the two systems continued alongside each other, on into the 1930s, eventually the more convenient and superior SOF won the day.

The odd thing about the old SOD system, was the speed of the disc, 33⅓ RPM, as with modern LPs. Due, so we are told, to the early experiments, when the gears of the mechanism happened to work out that way, with the film running at 24 frames per sec'. For some unknown reason, one of these discs ended its days in the window of the cinema lavatory. I remember it as very thick, and approx' sixteen inches in diameter, it was played with the needle starting from the centre and working outwards. The synchronisation of film and disc, was surprisingly very good indeed, providing the film itself hadn't been chopped about, by some ham-fisted projectionist. However slip-ups did occur, usually in the haste and confusion of changing from one reel (and machine) to the other.

A tender love scene enacted to the accompaniment sound track of a cowboy shoot-out, brought howls of derisive laughter from the watching fans, the not too adroit harmony of "Why are we waiting" was loudly sung with glee and complete lack of reverence to the hymn-tune, "Adeste Fideles".

The projectionist would shut down the "Simplex" and endeavour to sort out the mess. Bedlam broke loose, and only the stern intervention of the manager and the dire threat to close the cinema down, brought some semblance of order and sanity, to the unruly fracas.

I was about eight years old when I was first allowed to go, with the other boys, to the Saturday afternoon matinees. It would blow-in my pocket money (tuppence, when, and only when my father was working), but the sacrifice was considered well worth while.

With the coming of the "Talkies", many of the silent western stars, I heard so much about, and hoped to see, had disappeared practically overnight, their films were no longer in vogue.

Fred Thompson, very popular in the silent era, made his first film in 1921. With his horse "Silver King", featured in a string of movies, until seven years later, his career ended suddenly, under the wheels of a runaway coach, while attempting a very difficult stunt.

Bill Hart, the most famous of all silent movie cowboys, made his last film in 1926, and then refused to make any more, because he said, the studios were no longer interested in western authenticity. But he was already in his mid 50s, and admitted some years later, that he wasn't fit enough to carry on. He had no worry financially, in 1946 he died with over a million dollars in the bank.

Tom Mix, another western hero, was persuaded to join a film company, a business (in those very early film days) looked upon with some suspicion. He is reputed to have made 370 films, from 1910 to 1935. I suppose I must have seen him on the screen, but I cannot recall any of his pictures. The older boys dismissed him as a "fancy pants", dressed in gaudy cowboy togs, and not at all to be taken seriously. He bragged that he would die in the saddle with his boots on. The prophesy more or less came true, when in 1940 he wrapped his car around a tree, and broke his neck.

The Texan Ken Maynard was very popular with us boys. Came into the movies via the rodeo and circus. Clocked up 125 films from 1924. His last film was "The White Stallion" in 1946. He was a superb horseman, and acclaimed one of the best of the "B" movie western stars, by the critics.

But our favourite, in those 1930s, was Buck Jones, another rodeo rider. Started in films in 1919, but survived the onslaught of the "Talkies" far better than Mix. A very sincere actor, in a similar mould to Bill Hart. We boys worshipped Buck Jones, he epitimonised our dream of what a cowboy hero should be. Children are often very perceptive, and this was born out in 1942.

He was at the "Coconut Grove" night club in Boston, when suddenly the huge building burst into a ball of flame. Jones at first escaped, but time after time, rushed back into the inferno, to help others to safety. It was reported that 500 people perished that night, and one of them was Buck Jones.

Hollywood forgot him immediately, the newspapers had little to say.

Today he is just a forgotten shadow on a screen. The title of his last film was sadly prophetic,

– "Down the great divide" –

John Wayne appeared in a number of supporting films. How we loved these hour long bits of all-action nonsense, and cheered to the roof, when the title blazed on the screen.

"Monogram Films Present"
"The Three Mesquiteers"
Starring: John Wayne.
Ray Corrigan.
Max Terhune.

The casting changed at times, Bob Livingston appeared in some of the "Mesquiteer" films.

The onslaught of the "Talkies" brought with it another phenomenon, the singing cowboy. Gene Antry, a radio singer, started the ball rolling, as far back as 1934, there had been a few others about this time, including John Wayne who couldn't sing a note, Ernest Tubb filled in for him. Other singing cowboys soon followed, Dick Foran, Bob Baker, Tex Ritter, and of course, Roy Rogers (real name Lenard Sly) another radio singer. Gene Autry did quite nicely out of his movies and other investments, he was still counting his money in 1988 – a cool 100 million pounds sterling –

After seeing these westerns, we would charge out of the cinema, don a belt and cap pistol, then reinact the scenes all over again, with some heated argument, who was to be Buck, Ken, or Tex.

A toy cap pistol cost a massive sixpence, at the "Ark". I had to forego my western for three weeks to get one. The cast-iron barrel broke after a few hours, so I wired it together, but things didn't seem quite the same after that. We bought very few amorce caps, at half-penny a box, usually we contented ourselves with, "Bang! you're dead".

Next to the westerns, our second choice were the swashbucklers. Unfortunately these were mostly "A" films, shown in the evenings. Children were barred unless accompanied by an adult. The least expensive seat (at the evening performance) was fourpence, my limited finances, could never stretch to that extravagance. Mother had constantly rammed into my head, that tuppence and tuppence only was my pocket money, and then, only if the family provider was working. But there was one time she relented, and I was given a whole fourpence – riches indeed –

I stood sheltering from the rain, at the bottom of the cinema steps, until some kind adult took pity on me, and chaperoned me in. He deserted me, once inside, and I found my own way to the front forms, soon to be joined by a few of my friends, who had sneaked up the back exit steps, and not paid anything at all.

I really enjoyed that film, "Captain Blood" with Errol Flynn, this was his first Hollywood picture, and he was an immediate success.

On the following Saturday, we hung up our "Six-shooters", and raided "Pools" scrap yard for long narrow off-cuts of stainless steel, which we fashioned into fair replicas of rapiers. For many days the street echoed to the clash of steel, as we battled with each other, from one end to the other.

Films of Sherwood Forest, demanded another change of weaponry, Bows and Arrows now a "must". A suitable young Sycamore tree was finally located on the railway embankment, behind Bodriggy Street. It's supple branches carefully inspected and ravished, the bark stripped away, a string tied at the correct tension, and Zing! another terror was added to the street. Volley after volley of makeshift arrows, aimed at nothing in particular, flew in all directions.

The comedies were received with howls of delight, with Laurel and Hardy the supreme favourites. Heavy drama, love stories, and musicals, were dead ducks, many had a "U' cert" considered suitable for children, the board of censors obviously knew nothing of juvenile preference. In those pre-war days, we did have a ten minute break in the middle of the show. Confectionary and ice-cream, had not been introduced, so we spent the brief respite, going to the urinal, and generally raising mayhem. The older boys quietly contented themselves with a hand of cards.

Our Saturday matinees followed a pattern. We arrived about 20 minutes before opening time, ignoring the small queue forming at the front entrance, we raced around to the rear of the cinema. In those days "St Georges" had no rectifier to supply the DC current, from the mains to the projector arcs. A diesel engine driving a generator solved the problem.

The single cylinder "Petters" was not the easiest of engines to start. First, a plumber's paraffin blowlamp was applied to the vapourising plate, at the top of the cylinder. When this heated to a dull red colour, a handle was fitted to the large flywheel and turned with as much strength as could be mustered. With luck, the engine would fire, and chug contentedly away for the afternoons performance. But there were times it let us down.

Returning to the front entrance, we raced up the long flight of steps, handed over our tuppences to the lady at the pay desk, and stepped into the gloom of the cinema. A young girl was walking up and down the aisle, armed with a brass pump, squirting a concoction of scented disinfectant, over all and sundry. We suspected it was a creepy-crawly exterminator, but actually it was just an air freshener, and did neither.

The manager at that time was Reggie Tozer, a small man with a deformity of the shoulder, which tended to make him walk with a slight swagger. The projectionist was Reggie Virgin. It was said that the two Reggies never operated those machines, but had to fight them.

Having satisfied himself that the "Petters" was chugging away happily, Tozer returned to the projection box, via the centre aisle of the cinema. He could have discreetly, and unseen, walked along the corridor of exit steps, at the side of the hall, but this matinee walk had become a tradition, and he seemed to enjoy the acclamation of the young voices, "Hoo-ray – Good ole Tozer". We cheered until he disappeared through the curtained doorway, into his little world of creating illusion.

Today, with so much TV, the magic has gone. Our seats were the least expensive of all, and consisted of just three lines of forms at the very front. With luck, we might get into the middle form, but I often found myself squashed with numerous others, on the front row. We never sat on the rear form, this was exclusively reserved for the older boys. They sat there like ancient "War Lords", and ruled the "Spits" with an iron hand. Woe betide any of us that stepped out of line.

The "War Lords" were the bane-of-life to Jack Nicholls, manager of the "Star Tea" shop, unfortunately situated directly underneath the cinema.

On Saturdays, he would anxiously scan the cinema poster. If it was showing a western, he heaved a sigh of relief, but if it was a romance, or even worse, a Shirley Temple, he knew he could expect trouble.

During a break-down, and we suffered many, hob-nailed boots would beat a fierce tattoo upon the floor, and underneath, the "Star Tea" ceiling vibrated alarmingly. The first casualties were the gas mantles, and the manager watched in despair, as one by one they disintegrated into falling dust. But alas, his torment did not cease with shattered gas mantles.

When the film lacked violent action, the "War Lords" soon lost interest. One by one, they quietly left their form and stealthfully crept up the sloping floor, to the more expensive tip-ups.

Comfortably installed, they would, in their own words, "'ave a quiet piddle". Once relieved, they returned to take up their rightful place, in the "Spits".

The only floor covering in the cinema at that time, was down the centre aisle, the rest of the floor remained bare boards. Rivulets of urine, flowed unhindered down the wooden slope. In the "Spits" the cry would go up, "ere it comes", we lifted our feet and watched, fascinated in the

Our cinema, St Georges Hall. Circa 1914

gloom, as a stream trickled by, to disappear under the proscenium, but not all had survived the long journey to the beyond. Some had percolated through the joints of the floor boards, and found its way into the "Star Tea" emporium. With howls of dismay, Jack and his shop assistants rushed around, in a vain attempt to rescue the boxes of dried fruit, bags of sugar, rice and tapioca, from the descending putrescence. Finally with exasperated rage and utter despair, he charged out of the shop, and up the long flight of stairs into the cinema.

His entrance could only be described as a raging "Tornado".

Tozer quickly shut down the "Simplex", turned up the auxillary gas-lights, and reluctantly went to investigate. He had enacted the scene many times before, and he again promised, that if the culprits could be identified, their misdemeanour would be punished by a life-time bann. But of course none could be identified positively. "I know it's them s . . ." roared the afflicted, pointing to the back row of the "Spits", and the most angelic smiles, this side of heaven.

Deflated with frustration, he returned to the shop, fervently praying to his maker that no romance or musical, would ever again be shown on a Saturday Matinee. Shuddering involuntarily, he added, "And please Lord, never, never, a Shirley Temple".

Before "The End" flashed across the screen, the "Spits" suddenly erupted, and a uncontrollable flood of ruffians burst through the swing doors, down the steps, and out into the Square.

The (less than half-a-dozen) more affluent patrons, in the rexine and plush tip-ups, were the only ones left to stand respectfully to attention (almost weeping with shame) while the National Anthem scratched mournfully over the speakers.

Sadly Reggie Virgin died in action with the Royal Navy, in the far-east, during the Second World War. Other projectionists followed, Jack Cook, Ewart Hosking, and Dennis Baily, are still fondly remembered.

Reggie Tozer ended his working days, promoted to manager of a large cinema at Falmouth, a justifiable reward, to a very sincere and dedicated man.

I've asked a number of ex-shop assistants, their opinion of Jack Nicholls, the answer was always the same.

"He was a very good manager, ran the business like clock-work, he was strict, but tried his utmost to treat his staff fairly. Probably the best of all the bosses in the grocery trade. He had a very quick temper, but who could blame him? – with you young hooligans, playing your revolting games, in the cinema." – Nuf Sed –

Although over the years, the grocery shop changed hands, and banner, many times, it was always referred to by its original name, "Star Tea". For 60 years, a little gold star transfer, glittered on the glass panel of the door. Then some unknown, in his infinite wisdom, scraped it off, and another tiny piece of our history, was swept (with the dust) to eternity.

About the outbreak of World War 2, the cinema's projection box (now jam-full of equipment) had outlived its usefulness, and no longer complied with the safety regulations. It was dismantled, and a more spacious replacement of concrete and steel, was erected on pillars across the front of the cinema. It can only be described as a tasteless monstrosity, destroying forever the designed symmetry of the original tiled frontage. But bearing in mind the safety factor, the sacrifice had to be worthwhile.

Whoever owned the premises, must have had a rather outlandish sense of propriety, they renamed it – "The Palace" –

The cinema (like all others) did quite well during the war years, but the advent of Television, sounded the death-knell. The "Palace" struggled on, asthmatically, until the 1970s, when the arc lights flickered for the last time.

The old "B" westerns we loved so much, had died a decade before, of – old fashion sickness –

> – sorrows crown of sorrow is remembering happier things.
>
> Tennyson.

28

Salad Days

Salad Days – the days of youthful inexperience –

At 4 years old, I was still my own company. Children in the street were either years older than myself, or babes in arms.

The path along the front of the houses on our side of the street, was an extension of the properties. A few houses had their frontages walled in to secure their rights, but for the majority, it remained a sort of footpath, and, like the road, had over the years, reduced itself to an unrecognisable mess of ruts, stones, and clay. Outside No 22 and 23, a little more sense of propriety had been exercised, by laying the path area, with pebble-like cobbles.

One balmy afternoon, mother was wielding a broom and attempting the almost impossible task, of sweeping the cobbles clean. I was given a broken kitchen knife, and the boring imposition of digging out the moss, from between the stones. Not that I despatched much of the tenacious weed, but it helped to keep me out of mischief. Two ladies came walking through the street, accompanied by a little boy, about a year-and-a-half older than myself.

When Tom Allen sailed to Canada, hopefully to improve his financial lot, his wife Emmelene relinquished the tenancy of their house at Trelissick (the other end of town) and came to live at No 15 in the street. A property occupied at that time by her unmarried sister, May Kneebone, and her father, Richard Kneebone, a widower. With six rooms in all, No 15 was one of the larger houses in the street.

Emmelene and May paused to pass the time of day with my mother. The boy looked at me, and I looked at him, I can't remember saying much, but I suppose we exchanged a few quiet words, (in those days, children were not permitted to disrupt their elders conversation, an accepted discipline which did no harm, and probably did a lot of good).

We had just finished tea that evening, when the boy turned up again, and asked my mother if I could play in his garden. And so, Barrie Allen and myself became good friends, and have remained thus ever since.

Barrie being the older, was the first to start school, and it was he who introduced me to the weird and wonderful world, of reading and writing. I was soon proficient enough to scribble "dog and cat" and some other simple words, on any scrap of paper I could find. Now at last I was ready for the great educational experience, who knows, I might get to read my "Little Dots Annual".

Schooling usually started at five years old, I was still only four, to wait another year represented a quarter of my life, dark clouds of despair hung over my horizon.

For the first time ever, I pestered my mother.

"Why can't I go to school?"

"Why shouldn't I go if I want to?"

On and on, driving the poor woman to distraction. For the sake of peace and sanity, she finally capitulated and took me up the hill to Bodriggy School.

The school was represented by two beautiful, single storey, granite buildings, built only a few years before, in 1923, by "Jory and Sons" of Connor Downs. The Senior and Junior schools were separate units, end to end, but in line with each other. Elevated six feet above the roadway, buttressed by a granite block retaining wall, they looked very imposing indeed. A intervening border garden of Pampas and Palm, complemented the picture. Without a doubt, there was no other comparable "seat-of-learning" in the district.

I walked through the wrought-iron gateway with a certain amount of pride. My father and another carpenter, Syd Glanville, had hand-made all of those windows, and helped with much of the other carpentry as well.

One of the teachers directed us to the office of the Junior School headmistress, and a few minutes later we were ushered in, to stand before the great lady herself.

Mary Prahm was the most beautiful lady I ever saw, tall, slim, with the most gorgeous auburn hair, caught in a bun at the back of her head, it was still the fashion at that time. During all my years at the Junior School, I never heard her raise her voice, and yet she seemed to allude an authoritative presence, of, "One who must be obeyed".

My mother explained the situation, that I was only four, but was

Bodriggy School. 1991. Official opening, 8th January 1923
(photo: D. Philp)

slowly driving her around-the-bend with my persistent pleading. The lady looked at me and quietly asked, "And why do you want to go to school?"

Without hesitation I replied, "I want to read miss".

She considered the situation for a moment, "You know that children usually start school here, at the age of five".

Glumly I had to agree, my hopes were already crumbling.

"But", she continued, "I'll tell you what we'll do. You can come to school, if for any reason you don't like it, you can leave again until you are a year older, how will that suit you?" I can't remember saying anything, not even "thank you", but the arrangement suited me fine.

At that time the school was enjoying a short mid-term holiday, in only a few days, I would be enrolled as a junior pupil.

Then – disaster struck –

My bottom suddenly erupted in a mess of painful sores, the simple act of sitting on a chair, was purgatory, my hopes of going to school, were receding fast. There was only one thing to do, a visit to the doctors.

The old doctor examined me and smiled, "It's not infectious" he said, "but certainly very unpleasant for the little chap, it should clear up in a few weeks, I'll give you some lotion which will help". Mother explained the school situation, "Not to worry", he replied, "let him take a soft cushion along, he'll be alright".

And so the great day finally arrived. I scorned the idea of my mother as escort, at the age of four such shame would be unbearable. Barrie called for me, and armed with a feather-stuffed cushion, off I went.

The children in that first class, accepted me and my cushion, without as much as a titter, in fact no one took the slightest notice.

We sat in long desks, seating five in a row (the dual desks were installed much later). The class was sub-divided into two sections. Those that could write a little, were privileged with a stub of pencil and a scrap of paper to scribble on. The veriest beginners (ignoramuses like myself) were condemned to the far side of the classroom, given a slate and slate-marker, and told to amuse ourselves, by drawing anything we fancied.

The blackboard was directed at the "brainy" half of the class, but I could see it quite clearly, from where I wriggled on my cushion. Not knowing what was expected of me, I copied the one- syllable words from the blackboard, to the best of my limited ability. Half-an-hour later, the lady teacher made her rounds, glanced over my shoulder and said, "Here's one who can write some words, this afternoon boy, you will go to the other side".

So the cushion and myself enjoyed instant promotion, to the pencil-and-paper brigade.

I remember my second day at school, only because we were taken out into the quadrangle, for a folk dancing lesson – UGH – The very young like myself, started with "Ring-O-Ring the Roses", I felt a real twit prancing around singing,

> "Ring-O-Ring the Roses,
> A pocket full of tozies,
> Ahtishoo! Ahtishoo!
> We all fall down".

Nobody told me the word was "posies", not "tozies", I was middle-aged before I learned that this childish chant, was in fact, a sinister parody of the "Black Death". Obviously the teachers didn't know themselves, if they had, they would have passed out on the spot.

After about twenty minutes, we were regimented into groups and paired off to dance with the girls. This was even worse, in the street, little boys did not associate with little girls. I also had a problem with my feet, they never did what was expected of them. Perhaps the teachers noticed, I never knew, but after a few more disastrous attempts, they gave up, and happily I went back to my lessons indoors.

At the age of five, I was promoted to the next class, and it was there that I was introduced to the subtle torture, known as "The ink writing Pen".

These pens, designed by sadists, were about four inches long, with serrated, brick-colour, wooden handles. These handles were made deliberately smaller in diameter, than the average pencil, so as to inflict the maximum agonizing cramp pains, in the shortest possible time. I was sorry for the left-handed pupils, they were forced to write with their right-hand, for them, another turn of the "thumb-screw".

Each morning our inkwells were topped-up from a half-pint earthenware bottle, stored conveniently in a corner cupboard. Once replenished, we scratched through another day. Throughout my sojourn at Bodriggy School, the teachers unanimously praised my literary efforts, but one and all condemned my writing as awful, and with very good reason. A page of blots and splashes is not a pleasing sight. My suggestion that the pens were responsible, not me, was met with a frozen air and stoney eye.

It was while I was in this class, that I again came face-to-face with the harsh realities of this world.

Sitting next to me was a quiet, chubby, bespectacled little girl. Sums seem to frighten her, so I helped as best I could. The teacher turned a blind eye to this blatant cheating. I can still remember Jean Golden, in her neat brown pinafore dress. When she died, my little world fell apart, it was no longer "All things bright and beautiful", it was dark – it was ugly – it was frightening.

The long school building was divided into classrooms by two pitch-pine and glass sliding screens. Conveniently making an open assembly hall, at the start of each morning, then quickly converted into classrooms for the rest of the day. The screens were also pushed back for special occasions when the parents were invited, such as Empire Day.

Twenty-fourth of May was Empire Day, actually Queen Victoria's birthday (another useless piece of intelligence that was never imparted to the class, I doubt if the teachers knew). On the back wall was a large poster map of the world, with much of it coloured pink, and that pink bit was ours, the "Great British Empire". Other posters depicted peoples of all races, dressed in brightly coloured apparel, happily working on the tea-plantations, the farms, forests and mines, all part and parcel of our wonderful Empire, and underneath the facade of blissful contentment, all hating our guts.

What exactly went on at these auspicious gatherings, other than a few hesitant poems, inaudible readings, and ever boring speeches, I cannot recollect, except that I stood there with the other inmates, ashamed of my cut-down trousers, ragged jumper, and wiping my nose in a handkerchief re-cycled from the tail of a discarded shirt. I reasoned to myself, that if Great Britain owned all those faraway lands, what happened to my bit? Something must have drastically gone wrong with the system.

The years at Bodriggy Junior School passed by, more or less uneventfully, names of the lady teachers, Jordan and Opie, still spring to mind. My last teacher at the junior school was the unforgettable Phylis Paul Banfield (re-christened Polly by her pupils) a very strict lady indeed. Miscreants would be quickly brought-to-heel, by a swift crack on the leg, with a boxwood ruler. Angry parents beat an incessant tattoo on the classroom door, complaining bitterly that their little darlings, were being unfairly and brutally treated. Their rebuffs made no impression on that determined lady, children that misbehaved (and some that didn't) were quickly brought-to-heel regardless. My mother was quite philosophical about it all. "Don't come crying to me, if you get whacked, you must have done something to deserve it in the first place". So when I misbehaved, I took my whacks and silently called upon the fallen angel to wreak fiercesome retribution on my tormentor. But he never did.

There was one lad who had no intention of knuckling under. He was quite prepared to suffer the indignity of the ruler slapping, but no way would this teacher get the better of him. He bore his punishment without flinching, and continued to play-up, at every opportunity. But Polly still had a card to play. Catching him by the ear, she marched him out of the classroom and down to the first-year class, and remonstrated, "If you want to act like a little child, then this is the place for you".

Each day, from Tuesday to the Friday, he sat squashed in the little desk, writing "Dog and Cat", and adding up "One and Two", inwardly smarting at the giggles of the five year olds. The following Monday, crestfallen and repentant, he returned to his rightful place, truly having learned the meaning of the old adage, "If you can't beat 'em, join 'em.

There was one thing that we males appreciated, Polly Banfield allowed no favouritism, no sex discrimination, the girls winced and howled under that boxwood rule, just as the boys did.

In 1982 I saw Miss Banfield again at her flat in Penzance, where she lived with her sister. She was now a very old lady, but still able to get about, although she told me she had suffered three strokes.

Reminiscing about the old days, she said, "The poverty was appalling, I remember seeing two brothers fight over a piece of 'Heavy Cake'. I travelled from my home in Penzance, to Hayle, each day, a round trip of eighteen miles. Teachers worked a five- day-week, and my salary at that time was £150 a year". She looked at me closer, "I can't really place you, but then, I taught so many children, and about 1938 I left Bodriggy, to take a teaching post at Gulval, much nearer to my home. She paused, then a gleam of recognition came to her eye, "I remember now, you lived in the street, just below the school gardens".

With the School's Diamond Jubilee approaching in 1983, I passed on her name and address to the headmaster, and she was welcomed as a honoured guest at the festival. I had been looking forward to this celebration, very much indeed, but alas, it came and went, before I was belatedly informed about it.

Phylis Paull Banfield ended her days at the "Trecarra Residential Home" – Truro – and passed away in early May 1990. Interment followed at the Penzance Cemetery.

I still have one of her Xmas cards, she had added a footnote.

"I thought I had been forgotten". How very wrong she was.

But, back to the "Salad Days". My days at the Junior School had run their course, and reluctantly I reported for duty at the Senior School.

Headmaster Radcliffe had just retired, his niece took over the mantle of office, for a few weeks, and awaited the new headmaster, Mr Dorcie Pearce.

Richard (Dick) Penhaul was my first teacher at the Senior School. Everybody liked Dick, with the exception of Dorcie, and with very good reason. Dick was "Laurel and Hardy" rolled into one, life to him was just one big giggle, discipline was not one of his finer points. One morning he arrived late, to find his unchaperoned class in noisy ruction. Quietly opening the door, he crawled on his hands and knees to his desk, peeped around the side, and in a soft voice said, "I see, see".

The resultant uproar echoed through the building, the wood and glass partitions offered no soundproofing to that cacophony. The other teachers were soon loudly rapping in protest, and only the appearance of the headmaster, finally brought some semblance of order, to that unruly assembly.

Every day, something untoward seemed to happen in his class. On one occasion he spotted my inattentiveness, grabbed my exercise books, opened a window and flung them out. Too late, he realized that it was raining "Cats and Dogs". With a wail of frustration he rushed outside and retrieved the books, dumping the sodden mass on my desk, and mumbling apologies. I spent the rest of the morning trying to dry them out on the radiators. After class I sneaked them out, under my coat, and that evening my mother subjected them to a hot iron, a vain attempt to restore them to some semblance of their former glory, but without success.

The morning half-hour of dictation, was always taken from the gardening column of the "Western Morning News", a newspaper which seemed to have been his bible, I never saw him read anything else. Alas, with those awful ink pens, I usually gave up halfway through.

Dick's prowess at chalk throwing, was legendary. Chatterers and ne'er-do-wells would quickly be brought to order, by a carefully aimed piece of calcium-carbonate. But even an expert like Dick, could, and did, make mistakes.

Louis Bolitho sat in the next desk alongside me. One day we were indulging in a little natter, when a piece of the white-hard- stuff, whizzed down the classroom and struck Louis on the nose. His spectacles flew off, falling to the floor, fortunately not breaking. Dick was quickly on the scene, feverishly examining the glasses to ensure they were still intact, handing them back to Louis with some relief. "It wasn't you I aimed at boy, but him", he bristled at me through his bi-focals, then much to the merriment of the rest of the class, he gave vent to his frustration by boxing my ears. But it didn't really hurt, I didn't think he ever did anything to hurt anyone.

Dick was a dedicated gardener, and his secondary role at Bodriggy was, naturally, looking after the school garden, and giving instruction in the noble art of horticulture, to pupils who couldn't care less. After he retired to his home at Gulval, nothing delighted him more than to meet his old pupils, and have a few laughs about old times. But teacher Miss Banfield told me that some ignored him, and this, she said, "wounded and upset him very deeply".

Truly there will never be another like him.

It could hardly be said, that Louis Bolitho was born with the proverbial silver spoon. Both his parents died when he was only four years old. Luckily his aunt Annie Bolitho lived just a few doors away, on Bodriggy Street, and adopted the little boy. Annie was a spinster and ran a small shop from her back-kitchen, the few shillings from this enterprise, helped to keep the wheels turning. There was no money left over for luxuries, and like most of us in the back streets, presents for the celebration days (Xmas and birthdays) were very few or nothing.

Still she did all she could for the lad, and Louis presented himself at school, clean and tidy, more so than many of us.

As he got older, his aunt worried about the future. She had only a basic education, and no special talent to offer. How could she help? While he was still at school, she hit on a simple but novel solution to the problem. She gave him a ten-shilling note, it was all she could afford, told him to walk through the streets and collect a few small-grocery orders. Hardly anyone refused to help, Louis returned to his aunt's shop, and purchased the items at wholesale cost. With deliveries completed, he was left with a small profit. Each time he ventured out, he made a little more, it was a lesson he would never forget.

He left school at the age of fourteen, worked at a few different jobs, then set himself up in the grocery wholesale business. He lost some of his momento, when he was conscripted into the army, but returning to civvy street four years later, he re-started all over again, and became quite successful. Like myself he retired a little earlier than intended, through ill health.

Ever since our first day at school, we have been good friends, and when I reminded him of the ten-shilling note, he said, "Ah Des! I should have kept it and had it framed", wistfully he continued, "No mother could be more to me than Annie, I owe her everything – If you write about her – write something nice".

Each class had its ashplant cane, and on more than one occasion, I suffered the indignity of correction for some minor misdemeanour, and after two stinging whacks, I returned to my desk, with my hands tucked under my armpits, trying hard to fight back the tears.

The headmaster was the custodian of the "Flogging Cane", a massive creation the size of a walking stick, and probably a legacy from St John's Street School. I can't remember Dorcie ever wielding the awesome thing, but in times of stress, us boys were shown the beast, just in case our evil minds entertained any riotous thoughts.

Looking at the cane, I remembered the oft-told story from the St John's Street School.

Like all other schoolmasters, of the old days, Arthur Beavon (pronounced locally as Bevin) a burly ex-army sergeant, disciplined his flock, painfully and mercilessly, with many swipes of the "Flogging Cane" – Until one day – .

Young Alfie Evans suddenly stepped forward and with a well-aimed kick to the nether regions, floored the headmaster in agony. Only the intervention of the other schoolteachers, saved Arthur from further onslaught. It was now 1915, Arthur re-joined his regiment. The battle-fields of Flanders held few terrors for him, after five years with the St John's Street School.

Perhaps I was trying to emulate Alfie, when, during a playtime, Dorcie ordered me out of the cloakroom, and speeded-up my dawdling exit, with a kick up the pants. I rewarded him handsomely, by barking his shins with my "Seg" protected boots. The expected retribution never came, without saying another word, he limped away as quickly as possible to his sanctum and (I suppose) the First Aid box.

There was only one other time I openly rebelled against authority. Our woodwork master Mr Inks (Inky), ducked and avoided decapitation, when a Jackplane flew through the air, with deadly intent. A surge of temper prompted the attack, and I immediately regretted the action. He had always been fair to me.

Our very first woodwork master, was a skinny unsavoury character. He introduced himself, sitting with his back to the fire, his thumbs stuck in his braces. It was a cold winters day, while he stretched his legs on the table, we stood and shivered before him. He eyed us in silence for a few minutes, and then laid down the law. "I'm the boss here, if any of you scum step out of line, God help ya". We knew we were saddled with a prize idiot, and in retrospect, it was him I should have thrown the plane at.

Bodriggy School wasn't equipped for woodwork classes, so we walked the mile to Foundry and the Penpol School there. It made a nice break.

Frank Truscott was a well-liked teacher, and tried his utmost to make

St John's Street School, with Headmaster Beavon and pupils. Circa 1915
(photo: L. Penberty)

Remains of St John's Street School. 1989. Prior to final demolition 1990
(photo: D. Philp)

the lessons interesting. When the pupils' interest flagged, he called an intermission, and entertained us with one of his "True" stories, laced with more fiction than fact. It was during one of these excursions into the realms of fantasy, that a hand shot skyward. Frank glared over his moustache, not in the least appreciating this interruption to his verbal eloquence.

"What is it you want boy?"

"Please Sir – my brother said you're a bl . . . liar". With his ego completely deflated, Frank and the class returned to the curriculum.

Between the Dick Penhaul and Frank Truscott years, our learning was in the hands of a number of lady teachers. Names like Oats, Northcott and Delbridge, spring to mind. Almost forgotten now, was the lovely Miss Leverton, a statuesque beautiful teenager. The boys, who were by now, just about learning what "It" was all about, fell in love with her. Sadly she only stayed a few months, probably she was on a teaching stint – but, my word, what a smasher.

It was during these years, that I experienced my first real frustrations. No-one was going to take the slightest notice of the skinny "clever dick", in the tattered collar shirt. Sports were a nightmare, I had no idea of timing at all. When I tried to kick a football, I missed it completely. Cricket was just as bad, I reached rock-bottom in the eyes of my mates, when I couldn't even catch the bean-bag. This meant, of course, that I was never selected for any of the competitive sport events. I didn't mind, I was much happier out of it, and sitting on the side lines.

All through my school days, I suffered from flatulence, roast dinners, eggs, sausages and the like were absolute murder, and mother was constantly worrying, knowing that I was not getting enough to eat. My diet was mainly, bread-and-milk, some chocolate on bread instead of jam, and the inevitable chips, which for some mysterious reason, I ate with no difficulty whatever. During these years I was debilitate, and plagued with headaches and listlessness at the least exertion. Throughout my school days, my attendance was very good indeed, and I was seldom more than one or two days absent in a year. I simply told my mother that I felt OK, and trotted off to school. It was better than staying at home, bored to tears, with nothing to do. But there was one pupil in our class who had a much more serious problem to contend with.

Barrie Olds suffered from epilepsy, and it could strike him down at anytime, anywhere. I sat alongside him at times, for a second he fought against it, and then collapsed, often taking the desk with him. The teacher quickly organised a rescue team, and Barrie was taken outside to recover. Half-an-hour later they brought him back indoors, ashen faced and visibly shaken, and he was allowed to sit quietly at his desk for the rest of the day. He hailed from "Mill Hill" Angarrack, and walked to school each day, a round trip of two miles. I suppose he had someone to accompany him, but I have often wondered how often he must have been taken ill, while walking those lanes and back roads.

I tried to take an interest in the hour long, once-a-week art class. Our teachers knew little or nothing about the subject, so the exercise was a bit of a sham. We were instructed to draw "That". "That" being a single Tulip or Daffodil, stuck unceremoniously into a discarded jam-jar. None of my efforts showed any artistic promise, the flower always in profile, as in a child's painting book. During this hour of educational enlightenment, our teacher ignored us totally, burying her head in a union newsheet, thankful for the respite. But greater things were in the offing.

One of the lady teachers endeavoured to explain the "Metre Poetry". I rather liked poetry, although I admit the only poems I ever took any interest in, were from my father's American pulp magazines. Hardly considered good English literature, but it did spark an interest in that direction. I had tried to write some poems of my own, but lacked suitable material, inspiration, and the necessary talent. Now here was poetry that relied on the rhythm of the words (rather than the rhyming) to make the rendition complete, and musical to the ear. I accepted the challenge.

That night, I sat at the table by the oil lamp, and wrote on a piece of scrap brown paper (white was not for scribbling) my very first narrative poem. A cheerful little number, about shipwrecked sailors swimming to the shore, through a stormy sea, only to die, just as they reached the rocks.

"Blood flowed from torn splintered hands, frantically, hopelessly, clutching surf washed rocks"

I forget the rest, but I knew I had cracked it, with "Mother's Day" in the offing, my masterpiece would surely be prominently displayed for all to see.

The next day, I gave it to the teacher for approval, and requested that it should have pride-of-place on the open day. As she read it, her eyes dilated, and for some reason or other, her face assumed a grey, green, pallor. Then, as if in a trance, she muttered, "Er – we'll see".

The day at last arrived, and I proudly escorted my mother around the classrooms, displaying the many exhibits. "And what have you done?" she asked. Not that she was interested, she looked upon this side of schooling as "just kids playing around". I tried to explain that I had written a poem in metre, and it was good. "Well, where is it?" she was obviously getting more than a little bored. "It's here somewhere", I said, frantically searching the walls, but to no avail. A few minutes later she left me to my own devises, and walked home. It may have mattered little to her, but it certainly mattered to me. My glorious masterpiece had not received the recognition it deserved, what on earth could have happened to it?

The next day, truth was out.

A number of us were detailed to clean the pieces of paper from the classroom walls, when suddenly I spotted it. My teacher had fulfilled her half-promise, by pinning my poem two inches from the floor, on the skirting board.

I had yet to learn that children should only write about nice things, dogs, cats, flowers, etc, and leave the horror stories to the decadent adults.

On another occasion, the lady teacher voiced a brilliant idea. We were to be allowed to write a composition, on anything we wished, and to express ourselves creatively.

Dick Ingram (sitting just behind me) pulled out all stops and wrote, what only could be called a near classic.

"We went to the football match, but it rained, so we came home again".
The End.

Needless to say, his two line literary extravaganza did not meet with approval, and he was rewarded with a stinging whack from the ruler, for his impudence.

There was the usual outpouring of animal and flower stories, but I decided to take full advantage of my new found freedom, and write a rip-snorting western.

I had often listened to my two uncles, who had worked in the mines

189

of Montana, for some years. Their stories liberally interspersed with the most colourful language imaginable, so I considered myself quite an authority on the subject.

My ink pen scratched the opening words. "The Utah Kid gently quietened his rearing pinto, as a Side Winder slithered its zig- zag path across the dusty trail".

A good start I thought, it should be, I had pinched it from one of father's pulps. The rest of the story was just schoolboy imagination (or lack of it) until the closing chapter, when our hero finally catches up with, and confronts the bandit gang.

"Reach for the sky, you b . . . or I'll blow your d . . . heads off".

The next day, our lady teacher read aloud some of our offerings. When she came to mine, I saw the frozen, sickish look come over her face, once again. She murmured that time had run out, and no more would be read that day. As it happened, no more on any other day either. Strict censorship was reimposed, from now on it was to be, dogs, cats, flowers, like it or lump it. So we dutifully scratched away, and lumped it.

"Philp – come here – and bring that with you".

"That", was a copy of the "Illustrated Chips" I had been surreptitiously reading under the cover of my desk top. I had chuckled through the adventures of "Weary Willie and Tired Tim", and had now turned to the centre pages. I can only assume that her gimlet eye, caught my wide grin, as I revelled in "The Merriment of Casey's Court". Sheepishly I approached the sacrificial altar, a ruler snaked out and rattled my legs with a resounding smack. With pointed finger she mimed towards the wastepaper basket. Dolefully I deposited the pink pages, and returned crestfallen to my desk.

Our teachers had some weird and wonderful notions about suitable reading material. Childrens Newspaper, Boys Own Paper, and Chums, in that order of preference, with Billy Bunter just about passing muster. But these story papers cost a massive (at least to us) tuppence each, and available by order only. So we generally contented ourselves with the eight-paged penny issues, known in the trade as the "Penny Blacks". They passed from one grubby hand to another, until they eventually disintegrated. To enjoy a comic, it should be read by candlelight, the art work was fantastic, and recognised today as "The Golden Age" by numerous collectors. Although most of the comics of the 1930s have now passed into comic history, I still remember the titles with much affection.

"Chips" – "Larks" and "Jolly" on pink paper.

"Funny Wonder" – "Joker" and "Butterfly" on green.

"Merry and Bright" on mauve.

"Jester" on white, and many more, too numerous to mention.

To be fair to my teacher, she handed my precious "Chips" back to me as I was leaving the classroom, with the terse warning. "Don't ever bring it again".

I can only remember one story book at Bodriggy School, "Coral Island" by R. M. Balantyne. The weekly half hour of reading never progressed beyond the first two chapters, then someone would start playing-up, and the reading session would come to a full stop. A week later it was reinstated, from the first page, we never reached chapter three. How I loathed that book, even today I shudder when I see it on the children's shelves, in our local public library.

There was no library at the school, until the mid 1930s, when one of our patrons presented us with a number of unwanted tomes, from his resplendent collection. Needless to say, these books were totally unsuitable for children, but at least it was a step in the right direction. There was a County Library, of sorts, in a backroom of the Passmore Edwards Institute, but the rexine bound volumes attracted few borrowers, and one had to reach the ripe old age of fourteen to be a member.

My father was an avid reader, never more contented than when his head was buried in a American Pulp mag', "Thrilling Detective", "Black Mask" etc, tattered remnants of "John Bull" and "Answers" received his rapt attention. Anything in print was read voraciously, he was the only man I have ever known, that sat at the table and read every word on a sauce bottle label.

Reclining on a green table-cloth in the front room, was a combined edition of John Bunyan's, "Pilgrim's Progress" and "The Holy War", a massive brass bound tome, with metal clasps. Little interest was shown by my parents, but a vivid coloured picture of "Apollyon" fascinated me. The fallen angel in all his terrifying glory, breathing fire from a body covered in green scales, and waving a "Dart" in defiance at Christian. After looking at thst frightening portrayal, I suffered the inevitable nightmares, and mother declared John Bunyan out-of-bounds.

I wasn't too worried, the book was probably more rotten than "Coral Island".

Magazines never seemed to interest my mother, but she did jealously guard two hard-back tomes, that she read over and over again. "Castaways of Disappointment Island", a true story of shipwreck, and "The Mighty Atom", by Marie Corelli (circa 1896), about a little lad, an infant mathematical prodigy, driven to suicide by a domineering father. Desperate for something to do, I had read both books, while still only eight years old. Unfortunately, "Castaways" was lost forever, when borrowed by a distant relative, and "Atom" – well, who knows.

We looked forward to our five weeks summer holiday. On the previous colder days, we sallied forth with our "Butts" and raced each other down Brewery Hill, but now under the scorching summer sun, there was only one place to be – in the water.

With the tide out, and the Copperhouse Reach more or less empty, the veriest of beginners splashed about at Three Polar, (3 bends), a shallow river winding its way across the mud and sand flats. With confidence once gained they progressed to Yacht Pool at Black Arch, and from there to the twin deep pools at the far end of the Reach. When we spoke about Hayle Pool, it was these pools we referred to, not the Reach as a whole. The larger pool was deep and ominous, only the most stalwart swam there, the smaller one alongside, was much preferred, shaped like a sandy cone, a subsidence from a forgotten mine.

With the tide "in", the swimmers at the Copperhouse end of town, gyrated to "Dock Boards". The old dry-dock gates had outlived their usefulness, a lifetime before, left in an open position, and now firmly cemented in the silt. They made an ideal "Off" for swimming, the "Bully" (hinge) substituting as a diving board. The old dock was ideal for swimming, the water deep and inviting, the many swimmers saw to it, that no-one got into trouble.

But there was the ever present enemy – raw sewage – It floated on the in-coming tide, then finding itself landlocked at the dead end of the dry dock, accumulated there, until the water receded some hours later, and the loathsome mess again swept past "Dock Boards", out into the harbour and hopefully into St Ives Bay. Doctor Palmer waxed wrathful to the authorities, but his rightful protestation was ignored. We carried on swimming as before, avoiding the unpleasantness as best we could.

Across the grassy sandunes, and just a mile from our street, was one of the most beautiful beaches in the West-country, three miles of it. But for many school children, like myself, it was considered far too dangerous and out-of-bounds, unless accompanied by an adult. Every year, a solitary bell in the Church tower, tolled mournfully for some unfortunate. This was, of course, before the days of beach patrols and lifeguards. The beach life-saving equipment, was represented by a solitary ship's, cork, life-belt, staring from an open wood box, with its rope attachment neatly coiled alongside, but long since rotted to uselessness.

The beach near the bar looked so inviting, holiday tourists were drawn to it like a magnet. At the inner end of the harbour, lock- gates held in check the two large pools, Copperhouse and Carnsew. These were simultaneously released on the out-going tide. Millions of gallons of twisting, raging water, raced through the harbour, carrying everything before it. A simple, yet effective way of clearing a channel over the bar.

The sad story of Rubenia (Beany) Dennis, was often told as a warning to the unwary.

"Beany" was a beautiful girl from Ventonleague, she and her two friends, George Williams and Iris Harry, had enjoyed a picnic and a swim, on the Lelant side of the Hayle River. It was ferryman Tom Pomeroy who advised them not to swim again that day. George and Iris took heed of the warning, but headstrong "Beany" had other ideas.

A few minutes later there was a scream, she was caught in the rip of the current. George plunged into the water, and actually reached her, but the foaming torrent dragged her from his grasp. Day after day, the father, Charlie Dennis, walked the length of the long beach, hoping to find the body of his lovely daughter, but it was not to be. He tried to warn some holiday makers, who were swimming near the bar, only to be rewarded with verbal filth and mouthed obscenity.

Some days later, fishermen from St Ives found her body floating in the bay. At the inquest, the pathologist gave his verdict. "Beany did not die of drowning, but in panic choked to death, on her own vomit".*

The far end of the beach terminates at Gwithian, with its picturesque lighthouse perched on Godrevy Island, just off-shore. But the rocks and pools at Godrevy also suffered an unenviable reputation of many tragedies.

Gordon Andrewartha was limpet picking around the rocks, when

*The date of the Beany tragedy has been confirmed July 26 1923, she was 17 years old.

Crossing the Bar. 1940
(photo: D. Philp)

suddenly he slipped, and was swept into the water. His friend Arthur Hughes tried to help, and almost followed him, but to no avail. I don't think Gordon's body was ever found, he was said to have been a very good swimmer, but he just – disappeared –

At his home in "Companies Yard", a strange occurrence. His mother was busy baking in the kitchen, when suddenly, for no apparent reason, the oven door slammed shut. She hurried around to her next-door neighbour, and in a tearful voice cried, "My Gordon has just been drowned".

This frightening psychic awareness, was in-born to many Cornish folk. So the Three Miles Of Golden Sands, were taboo, that didn't worry us too much, there was plenty of water in the old dock, and only a few minutes away. Far better than walking the mile across the dunes to the beach, where the heavy surf made swimming not all that pleasurable.

All the old ladies in the street, were Grannies, whether related or not.

Granny Sampson was no exception. She lived next door at No 23, with her daughter and son-in-law, Rosy and Tom Pope. Granny was a short stout lady who ruled her small domain with a brittle tongue. I liked her, with all her resilience and assumed toughness, she was never coarse. I think she sensed a kindred spirit, and often we chatted in the courtyard.

" 'ere e are", she said, "maik a gud cowboy belt for e". It was one of those tight waist belts, young ladies wore in times long past.

"You waint believe it", she continued, "but more than fifty year ago, I wore that there belt, but – luk at me now?" I knew that she had little to give, she was offering me something she had treasured for many years, a fading memory, a link with the past.

What a grand cowboy belt, two inches wide, with a fancy clasp. It hung nicely on my skinny frame, but I often wondered, what she must have looked like, all those years ago.

"Cum 'ere", she grabbed me by the ear and painfully led me to the top of the granite steps, leading to the garden. Swinging me around, she pointed at three birds on the lean-to roof of her kitchen. "What do e see?"

"They're crows", I answered, brimming over with confidence and intelligence.

"You bucca", she rasped, "they got red fait and bakes, they there's Chaws, wun mus' 'av' los' 'is mait. Taik a gud luk boy, mae niver seen um agin".

It was the last time I saw them in the wild, although occasional sightings were reported as late as 1950.

As a boy, I remember the Chough pronounced in Cornish dialect as Chaw, and the "3 Choughs" pub at Treswithian, was simply referred to, as "Chaws Inn".

In the street, we weathered our mini-dramas as best we could, helping each other in times of stress and trouble. No-one else seemed to bother.

May Kneebone worked for the Mathews family, at their bungalow opposite the Swan Pool. One evening May returned to her home in St John's Street, and fell over the body of her father, lying in the passage. She, understandably, went into "shock", but managed to stagger to her neighbour and friend, Maggie Hamly, living two doors away. May's sister and nephew (Emmelene and Barry) had been visiting at Phillack, and were due back shortly. Maggie sent her young ward, Roy, into the street to await their home-coming and hopefully direct them to Maggie's for further information.

Roy was christened with the same names as his father, Evan Robert Owens, but the confusion was solved by simply calling the lad – Roy – . In April 1919, the ship S. S. Moss Rose, sank during a storm in the Bristol Channel, and Roy (who was only four months old) lost the father, he was too young to remember. His mother donned the mantle of bread-winner, and for many years worked in domestic service at Penzance. As was usual, in cases like this, the lad was placed in lodgings, and Roy Owens became the ward of Maggie Hamly.

Roy saw the mother and son turn into the street, and bore the sad tidings to them.

With May still in shock, incoherent and irrational, Emmelene realised that she alone would have to take over. She also knew that my father often officiated at funerals, so it was only natural that she came to No 22, to seek his advice. Father explained the procedure, and suggested that his old mentor Ned Coombe was a fitting undertaker. He also volunteered to go along and make the necessary arrangements on her behalf. Emmelene readily agreed, but after she had left, and on reflection, father wasn't at all sure he had done the right thing.

And therein lies a tale.

Francis Leonard Philp had served his carpenters apprenticeship with Edwin Thomas (Ned) Coombe, with home-base in the lean-to workshop, with its red tiled roof, on Glebe Row, Phillack. The work was hard and long, with little financial reward, but the experience was invaluable. He had started at two shillings a week, now nearly five years later, his wage was ten shillings, the going rate at that time. Ned had a habit of prefixing each sentence with, "Look 'ere look". This caused a great deal of merriment with the work-force, who mimicked the old man shamefully, (but, I would add, not when he was within ear-shot).

With four months still to go, of his five year stint, the apprentice decided to call it a day, and handed in his notice. A job at the Dynamite Works, with the dangling bait of a whole £1, was too good to miss. Ned stared at him in disbelief. "Look 'ere look", he stammered, "I was going to give you a bit more". FL couldn't resist a sarcastic repartee.

"Look 'ere look, cap'n, you're too late, I've had enough".

Ned was on the verge of tears, he had nursed this ungrateful wretch for nearly five years, hoping for better things in the future, now all his hopes had crumbled to nothing.

For twenty years, after that fateful day, the snub rankled, and Edwin Thomas passed Francis Leonard in the street as if he had never existed, the stone-face old man stared straight ahead, with no sign of recognition or greeting.

The Coombe family shop, on Fore Street, was closed, so FL timidly tapped at the window. Suddenly the door flew open and the avenging angel appeared. "Look 'ere look, what do you want?" spat out the apparition. Father explained the situation, and that he had recommended Mr Coombe, because, in his opinion, he was one of the best in the business. Ned melted immediately, the substitute for an apology, and with the peace offering of the impending contract, all was forgiven, the rift was healed. "Look 'ere look, I'll get the notebook, you fetch the tape from the shelf". Ned, with the notebook, walked up Cornubia Hill and into the street, the "Boy" bringing up the rear, bearing the large, leather encased tape, before him, like a Bishop's Orb. With all the care and dignity Ned could muster, the deceased, Richard Kneebone, was laid to rest at Phillack. As for father and Ned, they often enjoyed a chat together whenever they met, the wilderness years were forgotten history.

With the summer holidays now a memory, it was back to school.

The winter passed, more or less, uneventfully, but in the following year, I made, what was probably, my biggest mistake ever. The unfortunate psychological effect was a burden to be borne for the rest of my life.

The annual report, for top of the class, was monopolised by just three pupils, Janie, Ivor, and myself. Janie and Ivor were far more studious than I could ever hope to be, and usually beat me into third place, but one year, with the help of a kindly teacher, I pulled it off, and was acclaimed "Top" – Glory indeed –

With the Preliminary Exam' in the offing, Headmaster Pearce predicted that, at least, we three would be going to the Humphry Davy Grammar School at Penzance. Full of confidence, I allowed my name to go forward, and at noon that day I raced home, to tell mother the good news. I presented her with the form, and requested that she sign on the bottom line.

Mother did not seem to share my enthusiasm, but reluctantly agreed to sign. The solitary "J" gave up the ghost, she quickly solved the problem with a make-shift nib, fashioned from a matchstick, I tried to stop her – but too late. The indecipherable seal of approval, was firmly implanted on a paper, piebald with blots and splashes. Shamefully I took the desecration back to school and presented it to the Headmaster. He was not pleased, and handled the unwholesome thing with repugnance. "Still", I reasoned, "the exam is what counted, and I would be doing that myself".

After tea, that evening, my parents had a serious talk with me. It simply boiled down to the fact, that if I passed, they just couldn't afford to send me. Although the tuition was free, there was still so much to pay for. School clothes, the rail fare, and all the other things that parents were expected to provide and contribute to. I didn't have the courage to go to the Headmaster, and say, "It's not on, we've no money". There was only one thing I could do.

I sat for the Preliminary, and deliberately made a mess of even the easiest questions. Some weeks later, my teacher handed me the failed slip, in a sealed envelope. She didn't say anything, but her eyes said it for her. "Why did you do it?"

My mother could see how upset I was, "Never mind", she said, "don't take it to heart, you did your best", then as an afterthought she added, "If you had passed, we would have managed somehow". It now dawned on me what I had done, my ambitions to be a chemist or a teacher, were brought to nothing, if only she had told me before, now I had blown it. I never told my parents what I had done, I suppose they tried their best, but in those days it wasn't always easy. The psychological effect was that for the rest of my life, I would fall to pieces at the sight of an examination paper, no matter how hard I tried, or how well versed I was in the subject. In my adult life I scraped through a few exams, but failed more than I passed.

Janie and Ivor went to Humphry Davy, I stayed on at Bodriggy.

The following year, 1937, was the first time the school presented prizes. I had by this time, lost all interest in studying, but came 2nd in the class, without even trying. Mother beamed as I walked to the front of the assembly to be presented with my tome, "Play Up Royals" by Herbert Hayens. I promptly took it home and threw it in a wall cupboard. I still have it, in perfect condition, it should be, I never opened or read it, until fifty years later. It wasn't very good, hardly worth the trouble.

By 1938, our finances had improved considerably, and some of my school friends were making the transition to the "Hayle Grammar School". This was a private school, but the moderate fees were now affordable. When I voiced an interest, my mother amazed me by saying that I could go. (Did she find out about my Prelim' flop?)

I only stayed at the school for a year, not long enough to do anything worthwhile, but with stubborn diligence and perseverence, I came away with a very good report and a "Top" in my favourite subject Chemistry.

I can't say I liked it there, a régime of surnames only, and "adsum" in the mornings, did not find favour with my socialistic leanings.

At the age of fourteen, it was time to hang up my satchel, and like a lamb to the slaughter, I ventured forth into the adult world of – making a living –

It is sad to reflect, that more than half of my Bodriggy School friends, have now passed on, but at times I still see them in the shadows.

Oh, how I miss them all.

> "The old pals are always the best you see,
> New friends you can find every day,
> But they can't fill the places or ever be,
> Like the old pals of yesterday".
>
> From the song "My Old Pal of Yesterday".
> by Gene Autry & Jimmy Long. (Peer Music)

The author. 1994

199

I was visiting St Michael's hospital in 1966 when I saw this lovely old lady. The auburn hair had turned snow white, but that beautiful face, with scarcely a trace of age, was still easily recognisable. Nervously I walked to her bedside, she lowered her magazine as she saw me approaching.

"Hello, Miss Prahm", I said, "I'm afraid you won't remember me". She peered over the top of her spectacles, and smiled. "Oh, but I do – the little boy who wanted to come to school".

A few months later I was reading her obituary.

Conclusion

By 1940 we had moved from the street, to Ventonleague. As far as mother was concerned, it was back to her birth-place, but the old cottage, now extended, offered us much more room than our street house.

Mother spent her last twenty six years there, but her thoughts were constantly with the little house at St John's Street.

About a year before she died, I saw her engrossed over a piece of paper, she was slowly writing something in a large, almost indecipherable scrawl. Her eyesight, by this time, was very bad indeed. I was curious, she hadn't touched a pen for a long, long time.

"What are you writing Mum?" I asked.

She paused, and turned her blurred vision to my direction.

"These are the names of my neighbours in St John's Street,

— They were the lovely People" —

They turned aside and sought the dawn,
With all its trials and fears,
Who'll pay the price of sorrow,
When there's No Time For Tears.

Des Philp, 1991.